Praise for

WHAT'S NEXT?

"Kerry is a top-rate personal finance journalist . . . Smart, practical advice."   —Diane Harris, executive editor of *Money* magazine

"Kerry Hannon is one of the best and most experienced personal finance writers in the country."
    —Ray Goldbacher, money editor of USAToday.com

"*What's Next?* walks you through the nuts and bolts of switching careers so you can follow your passion the smart way and set yourself up for long-term success. If I didn't love my career so much, this would be my bible!"
    —Beth Kobliner, author of *Get a Financial Life: Personal Finance in Your Twenties and Thirties*

"Hannon's engaging profiles reflect the passion of those who have chosen to take a different path with their lives while her practical, how-to advice will make the journey smoother for others who are still summoning up the courage to take that leap of faith."
    —Tim Smart, executive editor of *U.S. News & World Report*

"Kerry Hannon introduces us to people who are making a success in their second and third careers—doing what they want to do. Hannon provides their testimony and resources for us all to use in the next phase of our work lives. Whether it's making chocolate or running a homeless shelter, the message is: If you want to be more fulfilled, you can be. An essential road map and guidebook, full of great ideas."
    —Jim Connor, assistant managing editor of CNBC Business News

continued . . .

"I wish Kerry Hannon's *What's Next?* was available in 2001 when I was laid off from my corporate job and left scratching my head, asking myself the question 'What's next?' Hannon's practical guide is a must-read for anyone in a career transition and life reinvention."

—Brian Kurth, CEO of Pivot Inc.

"Whether your motivation is a recent downsizing or a lifelong dream, Hannon's book is dotted with things to look at before you leap.... Useful advice for those who want to retool themselves after age forty... Peppered with ideas... Gives the basics on careers that best lend themselves to starting again." —*USA Today*

"Hannon has crafted her research on career transition into an important new book. It's an indispensable guide to anyone hoping to pull off a midlife reinvention." —*The Huffington Post*

"Full of insightful Q&As and lots of encouraging words."

—*More* magazine

"One of the best in this genre is by journalist and financial adviser Kerry Hannon—who offers specific and practical advice as well as inspiring stories to help anyone thinking about changing careers."

—AARP Radio

"Hannon provides practical advice on landing the job of your dreams."

—Jane Pauley, host of "Your Life Calling with Jane Pauley" on the *Today* show, sponsored by AARP

WHAT'S NEXT?

Finding Your Passion and Your Dream Job in Your Forties, Fifties, and Beyond

REVISED AND UPDATED EDITION

KERRY HANNON

BERKLEY BOOKS, NEW YORK

THE BERKLEY PUBLISHING GROUP
Published by the Penguin Group
Penguin Group (USA)
375 Hudson Street, New York, New York 10014

USA • Canada • UK • Ireland • Australia • New Zealand • India • South Africa • China

penguin.com

A Penguin Random House Company

Library of Congress Cataloging-in-Publication Data

Hannon, Kerry.
What's next? : finding your passion and your dream job in your forties, fifties, and beyond / Kerry
Hannon.— Revised and updated edition.
pages   cm
Includes index.
ISBN 978-0-425-27147-6
1. Career changes.   2. Career development.   I. Title.
HF5384.H364   2014
650.14—dc23   2013047400

PUBLISHING HISTORY
Chronicle hardcover edition / July 2010
Berkley trade paperback revised edition / April 2014

PRINTED IN THE UNITED STATES OF AMERICA

10 9 8 7 6 5 4 3 2

Interior text design by Laura K. Corless

To my sister, Pat Bonney, and my husband, Cliff,
with love and gratitude

CONTENTS

When I met the late John Gardner in 1995, he was in his eighties and going strong. Although hardly a household name today, Gardner had served with distinction as secretary of health, education, and welfare during Lyndon Johnson's administration. He created the prestigious White House Fellows program. He founded Common Cause, the first significant campaign finance reform organization, and Independent Sector, to provide a voice for the nonprofit world. A few years later he would help launch Civic Ventures and Experience Corps, to mobilize others in the second half of life to create a better world. There were many other ventures in between, along with a string of influential books on leadership, community, and self-renewal.

What I did not realize at the time is that he achieved all this after the age of fifty. For Gardner, the gold watch turned out to be a launch pad—the beginning of a new chapter that comprised his most significant achievements.

He is hardly the only person to claim such a trajectory. There are many other high-flyers who have gone from success to even greater significance. Former President Jimmy Carter created a more enduring legacy after his U.S. presidency. Al Gore's encore career earned him the Nobel Peace Prize. And when Bill Gates departed Microsoft he emphasized that he wasn't retiring. In his words, he was "reordering priorities," concentrating on the most important challenges he could imagine—ending poverty, curing disease, educating all.

As examples of these vaunted second acts proliferate, Kerry Hannon's wonderful and enlightening book *What's Next?* offers hope and help to the rest of us. It is a compelling reminder that the chapters stretching beyond Act I are something to look forward to—a time of new meaning, immense contribution, and continued income.

By addressing the genuine challenges of what continues to be for many a do-it-yourself transition, this book proves that the midlife shift to new fulfillment is not only possible but deeply desirable. It offers a set of compelling, credible role models and distills their insights and experiences into a reliable road map for successfully planning this transition. What's more, as *What's Next?* shows us, these uplifting encore opportunities are hardly exclusive to ex-CEOs and commanders-in-chief. They are within reach for anyone.

As you ponder what you will do for your encore, remember that you're in good company. Tens of millions of Americans are celebrating their fiftieth and sixtieth birthdays, making the shift from "what's last" to "what's next" more than a question of personal fulfillment. What millions will do next is a matter of national importance. How will we, as a nation, make the most of this talent and experience? How will we make it easier for the largest, best-educated, healthiest, and longest-living generations to create a better world for the generations that follow?

What's Next? starts the conversation by redefining success. I hope you start there, too. Then read this book for the encourage-ment, guidance, and tools to make your dreams—and the dreams of those you can help in your encore career—come true.

—Marc Freedman
Founder of Encore.org

INTRODUCTION

A New York investment banker becomes a small-town chef. A college professor becomes a chocolatier. An entrenched corporate exec accepts an early-retirement package and converts to the ministry.

Who doesn't fantasize about a second career?

Perhaps you've worked in the same field for twenty-some years and have run out of fresh challenges. Maybe you feel you have talents that are going to waste. Or there's something you've always wanted to do that's calling louder and louder. Perhaps, like so many others, you're simply worn down by the corporate routine. Or you've lost a job or were downsized and the frustration of landing a new position is pushing you to start your own business. There must be something out there that's more meaningful and more rewarding, right?

Marc Freedman, founder of Encore.org, a nonprofit that is geared to helping people start second careers with social purpose and meaning says, "People are searching for work that is fulfilling and gets them out of bed in the morning." While these work transitions involve following a dream or a calling, you don't want to get caught up in the romance of it all. "There is a blitheness that all you have to do is embrace your passion and the rest happens magically," Freedman warns. "It's not that easy. You don't open the doors to your bed-and-breakfast and the cheering crowds arrive."

Indeed, millions of Americans have already launched new careers midlife and every transition is different. In 2006, I developed *U.S. News & World Report*'s "Second Acts" feature—a regular column that looked at people who successfully navigated a complete career change midlife. I profiled people who had made such moves and featured their challenges and their motivations. Since then I've been fortunate to meet and counsel people from all walks of life, ranging in age from the early forties to seventy-plus, who have taken up a new course either full-time or part-time. Meanwhile, some have chosen to strike out on their own. Each one followed his or her own heart down a new path with single-mindedness, passion, humbleness, and an ability to live moderately. It's inspiring to sit down with people who are eager to start over in new ventures and find work that is more fulfilling. And why not try something new that excites you? The truth is, we're living longer, healthier lives, and that opens the door to all kinds of possibilities, and your next career could easily outlast your first one.

There are things, however, that can hold you back. First, money really can be a stumbling block. You may need to earn a certain salary to make ends meet. Or perhaps you have a genuine fear of outliving your retirement savings or are afraid of losing employer-provided health insurance.

Some people aren't sure what they are truly passionate about, even when they know they want to move in another direction. You may have a nagging feeling that when you start peeling away the layers to find your passion, you will come up empty-handed and discover that you don't have any exceptional skills and talents. Not so.

Other wannabe career switchers I have met are afraid to fail or, oddly, afraid to succeed. Yep. There's a huge accountability to success. You can't let up, and that can be hard work. And admit it, sometimes the thought that it's going to be all work can be a deal breaker at this stage in life. We simply don't want to push ourselves to the limits after two or three decades in the working world, building a career, meeting goals, and facing other pressures.

Then too success means change and the unknown. Enough said.

Even once you realize what it is that you want to pursue next and then overcome any fears about finances or insecurities about failing, after age forty, it can be daunting to start a second act. The mere thought of going back to school, learning new skills, or beginning at the bottom of the ladder stops many people from trying something new. And in uncertain economic times, making a major move is more daunting than ever.

Let me tell you, these are very real concerns, and I will help you work through any doubts to figure out whether you're ready to make a change. Career moves do not happen overnight. You might start working on a move today that you will make in a few years. Career change requires clear planning, market research, hard work, and a healthy dollop of confidence. It's a process. But dreams *can* come true.

The best advice I can give you is this: If you're feeling the calling to do something new, to find work that energizes you, gives meaning to your day and more, do it. Consider the old cliché that life is too short to be stuck in a dead-end job or dreading Monday mornings. Or if you've lost a job, have accepted an early-retirement package, or are a retiree or soon-to-be retiree worried about dipping into your retirement accounts and depleting them, don't feel defeated. This might be your opportunity to reinvent your career and redeploy your skills to find a job you love or to pursue a long-held dream.

In the following chapters, you will meet people who have made the big swing and love it. Each one tackled the new beginning with a singular approach. You too will own yours. You may not want to do what they do, but you will get ideas. I did.

You'll also find tips and advice on how to identify potential next acts, financially and physically prepare yourself for your next career, overcome setbacks and obstacles, network and promote yourself, and achieve success in your new role.

I'm certain you, like me, will be motivated by their stories to dig down and take the time to concentrate on your own goals and to tap into ways to shift your mind-set from thinking you can't to believing you can. I have in my career and continue to every day; you can, too.

As the Winston Churchill quote emblazoned in decoupage on the glass tray that sits on my work desk boldly says: "These are great days." Let's get started.

CHAPTER ONE

A Tough Cop
Turned Nashville Music Agent

To be the toughest female cop alive, you have to run three miles uphill, climb three hundred stairs, put the shot, climb ropes, bench-press, run a hundred-meter sprint, swim one hundred meters, and complete an obstacle course three football fields in length—eight events in one day.

Jill Angel has done that. And won. She captured the state of California's Toughest Cop Alive endurance competition for women and came in second in the worldwide event.

Don't be fooled by her five-foot-three, 120-pound physique. She's tenacious—and strong. For twenty-two years, Angel was a California Highway Patrol (CHP) officer, rising through the ranks from sergeant to assistant chief in Los Angeles, overseeing more than a thousand officers. It was a job she prized, and for a while, she was unstoppable. She witnessed the aftermath of countless horrendous traffic fatalities and was severely beaten by a drug-addled suspect.

Afterward, as head of the CHP's Critical Incident Response Team, she passed out at a shooting scene—partly from exhaustion.

Then it all fell apart. Handling nothing but the worst stuff on the Critical Incident Response Team for five years had taken its toll. Physically, she was spent: she had high blood pressure, migraine headaches, depression, and an inability to sleep soundly.

A single mom with two young daughters, aged ten and thirteen, Angel realized it was time to make a change. She handed in her badge and retired. But it was the power of music that really helped her turn the corner. And now she's in training to be the toughest music agent alive.

Angel has dabbled in the music business for more than a decade. It began on a whim, trying to help a coworker get her music heard in Nashville, where Angel's younger cousin, Ilene, an aspiring songwriter, lived. While still on duty, she began making monthly trips to Nashville, landing meetings with the heads of record labels and top producers. "Being an assistant chief at the time, I was determined to get through to people at my level. They didn't know what to do with me," she recalls. But she scored her ten-minute face time, and it made a lasting impression.

"People told me I would meet the worst people in the music business. 'They lie to you' and so on, they cautioned," Angel says. "I said, 'Are you kidding? I just spent twenty-two years as a police officer and was a commander in South Central L.A. The music people are some of the nicest people I've met.'"

While her fellow staffer never did land a record deal, Angel fell in love with Nashville and her cousin's music. "The more I listened to Ilene's songs, the more I believed in her talent. They gave me hope, especially in the dark days after I retired." She began pitching her cousin's work with a vengeance.

For Angel, it wasn't a big jump from serving as a CHP to pursuing the music business full time. "Both are making the world better somehow, though the two fields couldn't be more different in how they go about doing it," she says. And she can afford to be patient. Angel and her family can live on her CHP pension, which provides full health benefits.

Since moving into her new gig managing singers and songwriters, Angel has worked with a half-dozen artists, but her biggest success to date is her cousin. Ilene Angel's song "I Don't Think About It," sung by Emily Osment, costar of the TV show *Hannah Montana*, hit the Radio Disney Top 10, where it stayed for over four months. It went to No. 1 for three straight weeks.

Moreover, Nashville artists such as Dolly Parton, Tim McGraw, Reba McEntire, Wynonna Judd, LeAnn Rimes, and Kenny Rogers have put holds on several of Ilene's songs, expressing interest in recording them. Another protégé, Angel's nephew Matthew Angel, an L.A.-based actor and singer/songwriter, has finished his first album, and his acting career has taken off.

Angel called her mentor, Dick Whitehouse, a former record label head who has advised her for four years, to tell him she and Ilene were number one on Disney with Ilene's song. His response: "Of course you are. You're Jill."

And that's why she just might become the toughest agent in Nashville.

Author's Note: Jill is also now a certified fitness trainer working in person and virtually via online custom workouts offered through inerTrain.com.

I asked Jill to look back and share her thoughts on her transition to a career as a music agent.

What did the transition mean to you personally?

What drove me was wanting as many people as possible to heal from the music I was healing from at the time. My law-enforcement career had ended. Twenty-two years of law enforcement and I was really sick, completely stressed out. Multiple fatalities, line-of-duty deaths . . . after years of that I was depressed.

At the time music was really therapeutic to me. I started listening to Ilene's songs. I threw myself into songs being written by her and a couple of her songwriting friends. I found myself healing from their music.

Were you confident that you were doing the right thing? Any second-guessing?

I was totally confident. I actually craved trying to make Ilene happen.

Anything you would have done differently?

I would have been more selective about how I invested the money. I spent everything I had on it and at the same time went through a divorce that finished me off financially. So here I am six years later and very selective about how I put money into this.

You have to know where to spend the money and where not to. I learned all of that the hard way. It really does take firsthand experience *and* listening to other people. I didn't listen hard enough because I didn't trust most people in the business. I was so driven to make it happen myself. I was so confident. I actually thought I could make it in three months.

You can spend a thousand dollars recording one song demo, and everything my clients wrote I was having demoed if I liked it. There were also the costs of traveling back and forth to Nashville from California. And if someone said they would listen to a song, I would overnight it. A month later I'd be in that producer's office, and I would see my envelope in the corner on the floor with all the other piles of stuff not even opened.

I spent so much money. I didn't know once we had a number one song that it wouldn't bring in enough money to make my venture really take off. If I knew years ago what I know today, I would have a ton more money. Do I regret any of it? Absolutely not! I feel like I'm just beginning.

How do you measure your success?

There's so much soul-searching. How do we measure success? There has been a huge success with each person I have worked with, but the success and rewards have not been financial for me. Helping people make a living singing at gigs four nights a week, maybe not a record deal, but doing what they love and sharing their gift, that's an achievement. I did make some money off Ilene's number one song. Truthfully, at this point, I haven't made nearly what I have put into it. It has mostly been emotional rewards. I don't know how I can stop doing this, so I hope the money will follow.

How big a role did financial rewards play in your decision to make a transition?

None whatsoever. My goal was that I wanted my clients to have financial security. Very few artists get rewarded for their gifts. Not that I don't want to make money. I do. A fixed income at my age isn't really enough with young children. So I took a 20 percent cut for my kids' college tuition. But I was not driven by money. If I stay with my fixed income in retirement and pay attention to spending, I'll be OK.

How did your preparation help you succeed?

There were several things that helped get me started and keep me going.

First, I found a mentor who can answer my questions, whom I can bounce ideas off of, and who can open doors for me sometimes.

Second, I got my kids excited about it, so I have that support at home. They love it. I take them whenever I can. They love being in the studio. Now they are in performing arts schools. One takes voice lessons. One takes guitar lessons. All of this came out of my pursuing this endeavor. Neither one of them had any interest until I started doing this.

Third, I was confident. I may have overdone it, at least initially. I just jumped. And I learned as I went. It has kind of been that way my whole life. In the past, doors have opened for me. I learned not to be afraid to run through them. I've always been able to make things happen for myself. I looked at this the same way. At the time,

I was wrong because everything I didn't learn beforehand cost me financially.

What I didn't know also helped me, though. I didn't know that things that were happening for me don't usually happen. I'm so glad I didn't know that. There are thirty thousand songwriters in Nashville and here I was taking Ilene's songs directly to heads of record labels. These were people I shouldn't have been able to get a meeting with, but I just called them, and they met with me. It has taken time, but those contacts are beginning to make things happen now and will continue to in the future. I'm convinced.

What do you tell people who ask for your advice?

You have to have dreams or passions. You have to be willing to take huge risks to make big things happen. You also have to be sure of yourself and open to unexpected opportunities. It's not easy to outlast the challenges of starting something new. I spent the last five or six years throwing myself into this thing, and it is a very tough, tough business.

The business took off at first, then boom—I hit a wall. I almost gave up, and then this hot up-and-coming band came along called Tennessee Hollow. They wanted me to represent them. I heard their music, and I thought, I can't take on a band right now. I want to be done with being an agent. I have pretty much invested everything I have. I'm out of money!

But I had faith. I agreed to spend two days in Nashville and connect them to everybody I know. Some of the producers were heads of record labels! They were the huge people who took me five years to reach—and everybody I called took a meeting. It was forty-eight hours of the most effortless work I've ever known in my life. One day we were even at the home of the head of Sugar Hill Records. I had sent him a link and told him I really wanted him to check out the band. It was an experience right out of a movie.

By the end of it, I had three re-cord labels interested and a show-case performing live. Two labels challenged me to book a hundred gigs and develop a fan base over the next year. I signed a one-year contract with Tennessee Hollow and booked them as the opening act for a major artist.

> "You have to know where to spend the money and where not to. I learned all of that the hard way. It really does take firsthand experience *and* listening to other people. I didn't listen hard enough because I didn't trust most people in the business. I was so driven to make it happen myself."

What books or resources did you use or recommend others to use?

A book will get you started but it won't tell you how to connect with people. You need to experience things. Producers would take a meeting with me, and we always had a great time. Martina Mc-Bride's producer and I spent forty-five minutes talking about mo-torcycles—Harleys versus BMWs. He wanted to know why CHPs rode BMWs. The thing I love the most in life is connecting with people—and they remember me.

What are some of the surprises and unexpected rewards?

One of the songs I recorded saved someone's life. It's called "Time to Fly," written by my cousin Ilene. A colleague from the California Highway Patrol was suicidal. She bought the CD and played it all the time—and eventually decided not to take her life. If you listen to the song and the words you will see why. I spent six years and every penny I had, throwing heart and soul into that album. If all of that was about one person hearing that one song that one time, it was all worth it.

BUILDING A NETWORK AND PREPARING FOR SETBACKS

Shifting into a new career isn't always smooth sailing. You'll have the inevitable obstacles and setbacks along the way. We all do. But as Jill Angel's story shows us, one key to staying the course is having a supportive team behind you. Your cadre of supporters may include a mentor, a professional network of business pros, and a personal network of friends and family. Be open to their advice and suggestions.

Ultimately, decisions are in your court, but gathering wisdom is always a good idea when it comes to navigating tricky times. The more input you can get when a problem arises, the more likely you will be able to find your way to steady footing. Here are some steps to ease your transition:

- *Find a mentor.* Who do you know who might be able to guide you along your new path? Is there a college buddy, former colleague, or a neighbor who made a successful leap into a second career? Delve into your network of friends, family, and business colleagues. Tap into LinkedIn and Facebook contacts.

- *Broaden your mentor search.* If you don't find a mentor through your own network, get involved in your local Rotary club and contact the Chamber of Commerce near you to see if there is a professional association that fits your interests and expertise that you might join.

- *Seek out groups* where you can meet new people such as networking events held by your alma mater. Consider joining a peer group associated with your profession. Join professional associations and go to conferences. Take the time to go to special speaker programs, or workshops. I belong to the Transition Network. It's based in New York, but lucky for me, the group has a great chapter in Washington, DC, where I live. The group often hosts author talks and holds member get-togethers, including volunteer opportunities, play outings, and museum tours.

- *Explore volunteer work* that will allow you to show what you can do and build working relationships with a whole new cast of potential mentors.

- *Consider joining a SCORE chapter.* SCORE (score.org) is a nonprofit association dedicated to educating entrepreneurs and to the formation, growth, and success of small business nationwide. Both working and retired executives and business owners donate time and expertise as business counselors, and these mentors will advise you for free, in person or online.

- *Check out Senior Entrepreneurship Works.* Senior Entrepreneurship Works (seniorentrepreneurshipworks.org) is a site dedicated to workers over fifty starting new ventures, which may be able to link you up with a potential mentor.

There's also the America's Small Business Development Center Network (asbdc-us.org), a joint effort of the Small Business Administration, universities, colleges, and local governments, which provides no-cost consulting and low-cost training at about a thousand locations.

- *Ask for help in stages.* Don't be vague and simply ask someone to be your mentor. It's better to clearly ask for a small, easily delivered act of kindness, such as a virtual introduction to an expert who can help you. This may prompt him or her to continue to be interested in helping you again. Let the relationship evolve organically step by step.

- *Regularly consult or meet with your mentor.* Once you've found a mentor, take the time to meet and enlist his or her invaluable help behind the scenes in learning the ropes.

- *Prime your sales pitch for a potential employer or investor.* Your mentor can help you evaluate your skills and build your confidence and resolve. Then you can concentrate your efforts on what you do best—say, face-to-face meetings with someone in your network of contacts, who can then carry your passionate message forward for you. Or using your writing skills to develop a strong sales proposal.

- *Be prepared for setbacks.* Starting a new business in uncharted territory or transitioning into a new career takes time. It could take off like gangbusters, but in time, you will hit inevitable setbacks. This not only will require internal fortitude but also will force you to ask others who know the ropes for help and guidance. This is when a solid mentor by your side comes in handy.

- *Seek and listen to advice from people who have been successful in the field.* They can help you find leads when you're ready to get your foot in the door, but more important, they can give you a real sense of what their work is like on a day-to-day basis. Use their advice to get a sense of what has brought them success and what stumbling blocks to avoid as well what opportunities might be out there for someone with your background.

- *Don't be defensive.* When you ask for pointers, be prepared to listen carefully and put your emotional reactions aside. Remember that a critique is all about improvement.

- *Tap into your personal network.* You never know who can bring you clients or help you build your business. Reach out to potential contacts through alumni publications, websites, or regional associations, if there's a chapter near you.

- *Say thanks.* Write thank-you notes and look for other simple ways to express your appreciation when someone goes out of his or her way to support you. It works wonders in building relationships.

Meet Your Virtual Mentor

I met John Spence a few weeks ago. He was smart, funny, generous with his advice, and encouraging. I didn't actually meet him with a handshake but rather a big smile and hello via my laptop screen one morning. He was at his desk in Gainesville, Florida, and I was in my home office in Washington, DC.

Our visit was arranged via PivotPlanet (pivotplanet.com), a virtual mentoring service, founded by Brian Kurth, author of *Test-Drive Your*

Dream Job: A Step-by-Step Guide to Finding and Creating the Work You Love. PivotPlanet lets you connect with expert advisers via one-on-one video and phone conferences. More on how this works in a minute.

We talked for an hour. John is a professional speaker and author of *Awesomely Simple: Essential Business Strategies for Turning Ideas into Action*. His client list includes such top-drawer outfits such as Apple, GE Capital, AT&T, IBM, and PepsiCo.

He delivers speeches to an average of thirty thousand people each year mostly around the topic of leadership. Largest audience: eight thousand.

And he makes an enviable income doing it.

Why I needed a virtual mentor. Here's why I sought his help. I had a newly published book, *Great Jobs for Everyone 50+: Finding Work That Keeps You Happy and Healthy . . . and Pays the Bills*, and was eager to get the word out and teach and inspire experienced job hunters on ways to land a job today.

Sure, I've been a speaker on numerous occasions over my career to a wide range of audiences from my Shady Side Academy high school alumni group and four-hundred-plus student assembly to the high-powered Executive Women in Government audience to a group of experts at the Federal Reserve Bank in Kansas City to a large gathering of corporate board of directors at their annual meeting. I deliver advice gleaned from my personal finance and career books, but I was ready to really pump it up to the next level.

I have a few mentors that I regularly turn to for help and advice, but this time I had a very specific area of expertise I was seeking to tap for guidance. I felt I needed some help from an expert on how to raise my profile as an expert professional speaker. I didn't have anyone to turn to for counsel in my own networking wheelhouse whom I felt comfortable asking. So I decided to test out PivotPlanet's mentoring service. We all need someone with experience and gravitas of whom we can ask questions without fear of looking stupid or putting our position in jeopardy. But sometimes finding an unpaid adviser, however, who has the time available to listen and counsel takes time and patience.

Virtual help. For the sake of time and desire to learn from one of the best on the circuit today, I was prepared to pay for counsel. John Spence's willingness to sit down with me, a stranger, for an uninterrupted hour was a time-saver for me but also let me make a connection with someone I may never have met otherwise. I suspect, I may learn more from him over time.

And that's precisely what PivotPlanet has in mind. The mission of the new service is to offer easy access to expert advisers in hundreds of fields from acupuncture to financial planning to landscape design and more to people looking to "pivot" from an existing career to another. "It's networking and counseling for job seekers of all stripes— from aspiring entrepreneurs to people burned out in the corporate cubicle, and baby boomers planning encore careers," Kurth says, "at a fraction of the cost of hiring a career coach."

My session with Spence was billed at $120. But there are sessions with, say, a vet tech for $54 an hour. You can set up a PivotPlanet account and link it to your Facebook or LinkedIn profile—it's that easy.

Once you have confirmed a time to connect with your mentor, have a list of questions ready to go and a pad and pen for note taking. Pivot-Planet is designed to help build a more concrete mentor relationship that can evolve over a series of sessions at regular intervals and on an as-needed basis. For me, Spence hit it out of the park. I can't attest for other advisers, but my experience was a good one.

CHAPTER TWO

A Cross-Country Journey from News to Wine

Becoming a wine maker—never mind a wine maker in Walla Walla, Washington—had never crossed Steve Brooks's mind. Then he stumbled upon a *New York Times* story about the fast-growing wine industry in the tiny verdant town near the Blue Mountains.

That chance reading came at an opportune time. Brooks, then a veteran TV producer at CNN in Atlanta, was growing disillusioned with the gloom of the news business and the strains of his perpetual travel schedule. After a nineteen-year career at the cable network, Brooks, at the age of forty, took a buyout. He had met his wife, Lori, at CNN and traveled the world covering news stories. "The finest part of those typically long days in the field was enjoying the local wine and trading stories with colleagues," Brooks recalls.

The article sparked a yearning to make a change in his life and his family's. "I missed spending time with my wife and two daughters, then ages two and seven. In the back of my head, I knew I had to find something else to do. I didn't want to stay there for another twenty years and be grumpy and unhappy," he says.

Brooks had never before made wine or even studied wine making. "Plus, I thought only multimillionaires could afford to own a winery," he says. Living in a town like Walla Walla, with around thirty thousand residents in the remote southeastern corner of Washington State, was far from his mind. He had never even heard of it. But after talking the scheme over with his wife, Brooks told everyone he knew that he was going to start his own winery. "That way, I couldn't back out of it," he says with a laugh. "At CNN, I was always confident that I could do as good a job as anyone else," he adds. "Why couldn't I take that faith in myself to another career? Every other wine maker in the world started out at the same spot . . . knowing nothing."

So the couple quit their high-paying jobs, sold the family home, packed the kids into their Volvo wagon, and headed to the Pacific Northwest to start fresh in a town where they knew nary a soul. Brooks enrolled in the local community college's Center for Enology and Viticulture for the hands-on study of every stage of wine making, from planting the vines to harvesting, fermenting, and bottling. He also worked as an apprentice to top-drawer wine makers in the region.

Finally, he began to make his own wine, buying grapes from established Washington State vineyards. "I couldn't afford to buy land and still can't," he says. "That's a gigantic investment. It's not like growing carrots." Instead, Brooks finds the best fruit to buy and determines when the grapes are ready to be picked. Vineyard laborers harvest the grapes, and Brooks hauls them back to a leased building outfitted with top-of-the-line equipment to work his magic.

Brooks is a one-man shop. But he's quick to ask the advice of veteran vintners. "People here are very sharing of their information," he says. "I wanted to make a rosé. I called up a wine maker I admired and said, 'If I buy you lunch, can you tell me how you did it?'" He did.

"For the first Syrah blend I put together, I changed my mind so many times it was silly," he says. "I asked a friend who has made plenty of well-received wines for his opinion—at least three times. Then, at the last second, I did what my gut told me to do and didn't listen to anyone else. The Syrah got ninety points [out of a hundred from a respected wine reviewer]."

In 2013, production was up to around three thousand cases; double that of four years earlier. Retail prices range from $16 for a rosé of Cabernet Franc to $40 for a half bottle of Sémillon ice wine. Brooks's wines are sold in more than 125 outlets in ten states (including Washington, Oregon, Idaho, and Georgia) and a few countries (mainly Canada and Japan). And he sells online through Amazon and the winery's own site.

The number of folks who are interested in starting a winery have dwindled since the economic meltdown, but when they ask, I try to dissuade them, Brooks says. "This is a business that demands lots of capitalization up front, or you are always struggling to catch up. I am doing a lot of things right, but it is still hard."

"As far as work goes, even a bad day here is better than a good day in the news business," he says with a smile.

For now, Brooks pours the bulk of revenues back into the growing business, although he does pay himself a salary. And Brooks exudes a laid-back confidence that it will continue to succeed: "I feel like I will never ever know everything there is to know . . . but I have a good product, thanks to the training I had from wine makers at the top of their profession."

Trust is what his journey from news producer to wine maker is about, and it's also the name of his winery: Trust Cellars. And Brooks shares that philosophy with his customers in a message on his wine bottle labels: "To change, to shift. To make an about-face. To move from a lifestyle rooted in technology and speed to an existence focusing on soil and sun. Taking a giant step requires trust. The trust of your family and friends . . . and the trust in yourself."

I asked Steve to look back and share his thoughts on his transition to wine making.

What did the transition mean to you personally?

It wasn't a touchy-feely thing. I just knew that I wanted to do something else before I died—I was bored with what I was doing, and there had to be something else out there that was more fulfilling.

In television, even though the on-screen correspondents get all the praise, in reality forty or fifty people are behind them doing everything. I wanted to do something that was just me, for which everything wasn't a group decision. There were so many things I felt got watered down to the point at which they weren't very exciting ideas anymore. I wanted to try something that was all mine—either good or bad—I was the one responsible for it.

Were you confident that you were doing the right thing? Any second-guessing?

There are times when I second-guessed whether it was really possible to make a living. And sometimes I still think, Wow, am I really ever going to get big enough to provide for everybody? It takes patience or plenty of up-front capital. If I'd started with a lot of money, I'd be better off, no doubt.

But even with money, I'd still have to build the brand name and reputation. Since I'm not a stock car driver or a golfer with name recognition, I wasn't going to release twenty thousand cases of wine and expect to sell it all in a year's time as I needed to. I had to start smallish and build and build and build.

Anything you would have done differently?

There are little things, but to be honest, not really. I wish I had saved up more money and started with more capital. It is not safe and easy to head off on your own. And I missed those benefits and that paycheck every two weeks. But I would do it again, that's for sure. I'm pretty happy with how things unfolded.

How do you measure your success?

I figure there are two things you can look at—sales and reviews. They don't always equate. Reviews are all over the place. I have submitted the same wine and gotten everything from great reviews to "not recommended." A better measure for me is sales. People talk with their wallets. If you can sell wine to people in the tasting room where they're trying it, that's good. Last year our profit was up pretty close to threefold. Still not huge numbers, but I can tell it is going in the right direction.

How big a role did potential financial rewards play in your decision to make a transition?

Money was not a motivator for me. It helped, of course, that Lori was still pulling in a good income from her freelance work as a TV sports director. Having a partner to share the financial load during these start-up years is an important piece of why I am able to take on this second act.

How did your preparation help you succeed?

You have to get your family on board with your dream. You can't do it otherwise. Especially for something as drastic as moving across the country. Our kids weren't crazy about it, but they are glad now.

Second, I didn't just say I was going to start a winery and boom it was off and running. It took three years to get here. During those years we were spending a lot of time looking at property, trying to figure out where to go.

The best part was that once I got here, I was able to learn firsthand what the job was all about by working for other wineries and vineyards. That was the best training. I actually got paid at some of them, although it was minimum wage. I was a cellar rat, and I did that for three years off and on. During that time, I was putting my business plan in place. I took pertinent classes—the science of wine making and vineyard management at the local community college's Center for Enology and Viticulture.

What do you tell people who ask for your advice?

I tell them to first find out what it is really like. Specifically to wine making, people think it is glamorous, and it's awesome, and all you do is sit around and drink wine all day. Like many other jobs, that's not the reality, and it's important for people to know. Take a "work-cation." Working vacations let you set up for a few days at a winery, a B&B, or something that you think you really want to do. You find out what it is like working at those jobs even if it's for a brief time. Chances are the reality is nothing as enchanting as what it seems.

> "I was always confident that I could do as good a job as anyone else. Why couldn't I take that faith in myself to another career?"

Is spending more time with family a bonus?

Well that was originally part of the idea! Right now I work more than I did before, way more. I honestly didn't think that was possible. I very rarely take weekends off. During harvest it can be twelve to sixteen hours a day, seven days a week for six to eight weeks. The rest of the year it seems to be usually eight- or ten-hour days, but that's still seven days a week. I'm not complaining at all, though—for me, even the longest day at the winery is far better than the shortest day before at CNN.

What are some of the surprises and unexpected rewards?

I have certainly met a lot of people who are very fun and very cool. That is really the best part of it, hanging out in the tasting room all weekend and meeting people from all over the country. It is not something I ever really thought about ahead of time. And I have gotten some really good reviews that I didn't think I would get this early.

FORM A CAREER CHANGE CLUB

I adapted the following tips from PivotPlanet's pro Brian Kurth, who encourages clients to join a group of other people who are looking to make a change. The members can run the gamut from being unfulfilled in their work, unemployed, or completely burned out in their current jobs. When forming a group keep the following in mind:

- *Start recruiting members by talking to your friends and coworkers.* Consider posting flyers at gathering places, such as coffee houses, civic organizations, churches, play groups, libraries, and health clubs.

- *Keep it small.* Suggested membership: A minimum of four and maximum of twelve.

- *Set a meeting place and time.*

- *Plan topics to discuss*, such as define a great job, and address fears such as financial instability, family disruption, giving up an identity, and failing at something new—all possible stumbling blocks to a successful career transition.

- *Write action plans and lists of all the things you need to learn and do in order to realize a great new job.* Be accountable to each other for your accomplishments each week.

- *Brainstorm about ways to find a mentor.* Having a mentor is at the heart of a successful career transition.

Defining How You Plan to Measure Success

Before you even begin your new venture, you need to get real with yourself. Dreams and dream jobs are attainable, but keep them in perspective. Here are some considerations to help you keep your feet firmly on the ground:

- *Be realistic about your expectations.* You can't go into a new biz expecting a strong profit right off the bat. You have to be content knowing that the pleasure will come from what you're doing and not from how much you're making.

- *Have your support team in place.* No one else needs to own your dream, but they do need to have your back when things get rocky. No one escapes challenges. Having someone like a spouse, mentor, best friend, sibling, or even an adult child to talk to is hard to put a value on, but it makes a difference emotionally. It can keep you centered and moving forward one step at a time.

- *Keep a gratitude list of intangible income.* These are moments of connection with customers. The freedom to not ask permission to take the day off to spend with your eighty-four-year-old mother on her birthday. The wonder of losing yourself utterly in the zone of your work. This is your special currency. Recognize it. Enjoy it. And be grateful for it. That's income that's tax-free.

- *Say it: "Nothing is forever."* Don't get stuck by the notion that this act is your final one. And if you don't hit it out of the ballpark, you are less than. Not so. Chances are you may move onto something different in five or ten years. You might have to. Lots of people do. Who knows? There are plenty of future changes that we can't control or foresee, so strive to be resilient and flexible.

- *Stay poised for adventure.* Trying different paths is part of the human experience. Don't let yourself feel trapped by this act. Keep learning new things. Revel in your new career for today, but always keep a plan for the future and be willing to try new things—always. That's what makes our lives rich.

CHAPTER THREE

From Stress to Bliss

When Lisa Eaves meets new patients, they inevitably ask: "Do you have kids?" And when she says no, their knee-jerk response is, "Why are you doing this?"

Eaves is a licensed acupuncture therapist in Washington, DC, who specializes in fertility and women's health issues. She's the sole proprietor of Heal from Within acupuncture and the Mind/Body Fertility Program of DC. The bulk of her practice is treating women who are trying to get pregnant.

"I love children but never imagined having any of my own," she says. "It seemed like a good balance to me—not bringing any children into the world myself, I spend my time helping other people do so."

Eaves's softly lit office oozes a New Agey ambience, from the background music wafting through the space to a richly woven rug hanging on the wall, flickering candles, and a bowl of smooth stones.

A very Zen-like aura lingers. It's the antithesis of her once hard-charging world as a highly ranked technical support manager at Fannie Mae, where it was not unusual for Eaves to be tied to her beeper 24/7. "I was incredibly driven, constantly in the office working," she recalls.

She was rewarded with a salary nearing six figures and all the benefits. But she burned out. "There is a price you pay for staying where you are. It kills your spirit after a while."

Eaves's spirit and approach to life have always been nontraditional—evolving over time. After high school, she barnstormed the country, playing outfield on a women's softball team. "My education was on the road," she says, laughing.

In the off-season, she pieced together college credits at the University of Louisville, close to her Kentucky childhood home. Finally, at twenty-seven, she headed east. She finished her bachelor of science degree in business at the University of Maryland in 1987 and quickly landed a job managing contracts for a firm building turnkey systems for the U.S. Department of Defense.

During that time, Eaves was diagnosed with melanoma. "It was really scary to have the big C," she recalls. She began doing meditation and looking for teachers. She went to different churches trying to find answers. With the original melanoma, they removed about ten square inches from her back. There was no chemo or radiation. It had nothing to do with stress, she says. "I believe youthful sunbathing was the primary contributor." There have been two more bad patches since, all surgically removed without chemo or radiation.

In 1993, she accepted a position at Fannie Mae and quickly became immersed in her work. At the time, a friend was studying acupuncture. Eaves was curious about how it might help her deal with her work stress but pushed it aside, until she faced the milestone of turning forty. A two-week rafting trip through the Grand Canyon stirred things up. She spent her time off the river keeping a journal and losing herself in the beauty of the landscape and in her thoughts. "It was unsettling," she recalls. "I was going to be forty. I was alone. My family was far away, and I was trying to figure out what I was doing here."

When she returned to Washington, she started reading about Chinese medicine, made acupuncture appointments for herself, visited the Maryland Institute of Traditional Chinese Medicine, and enrolled in classes. She both worked and went to school full time, but eventually she began working three days a week. After graduation, she started a part-time practice but held on at Fannie Mae for four more years.

Financially, Eaves has made it work by living simply and always putting money away. In addition, she had saved carefully before heading off on her own, built up a healthy 401(k), and accumulated a respectable amount of Fannie Mae company stock.

Today, her practice pulls in more revenue than she was making at Fannie Mae. There are marketing expenses, rent, a bookkeeper, health insurance, and funding her retirement, but she is making a better living than she was in her corporate days.

Eaves sees more than thirty patients a week, in addition to her mind/body workshops. "I coach these women," she says. "Acupuncture is just the tip of it. It's not just a physical treatment. You really tap into people's energy and their spirit. It's a little lightning rod to the human spirit."

In her workshops, she teaches stress-reduction techniques and ways to harness inner strength through meditation, yoga, and nutrition.

The group discusses stress hormones that are in the bloodstream when a woman is going through fertility treatment. "It's right up there with people having been diagnosed with cancer and other life-threatening diseases," Eaves says. That anxiety "challenges everything you have ever thought about yourself and your marriage, your spouse, your relationship with God, and who you are. It's a very isolating experience that brings everything to the surface. My goal is for my patients to be at peace, whatever the outcome is."

———

I asked Lisa to look back and share her thoughts on her transition to a career as an acupuncturist and healer.

What did the transition mean to you personally?

I was turning forty and had taken a trip through the Grand Canyon, which really opened up my heart to possibilities. That was a milestone. And I felt unsettled at Fannie Mae every day. It just wasn't doing it for me. I was kind of surprised I was there anyway because I am not technical. I had to work so hard because things did not come easily for me. I just couldn't stay there. I had to go.

As I started taking courses, I began to look inside and answer some important questions: What am I best at? What are my gifts? Today, I know. Working with people is easy. I love it. I love starting the healing process for others.

Were you confident that you were doing the right thing? Any second-guessing?

The only time I felt uncertain was the first thirty days after I quit Fannie Mae completely. It was so scary. All the safety nets were gone. No money was going to appear magically in my checking account every two weeks. No health benefits. No stock options. But almost magically after a month, I realized, It's going to be OK. I could do this.

Anything you would have done differently?

I don't really know how I could have done anything differently because I made decisions based on what I knew at the time. I took it in incremental steps: I graduated. I got my license. I started treating people part-time. I ramped up my practice to full speed.

How do you measure your success?

It's pretty simple—I love to go to work. I never said that before. I love to go to my office. The money is a motivator, but it is not primary. That is one of the bonuses. I feel successful because I love what I am doing, and I think I make a difference in other people's lives.

How big a role did financial rewards play in your decision to make a transition?

I never really thought I was going to make much money. I thought, if I could make as much money as I was making at Fannie Mae, I'd be happy. I'm actually making more, which is even better!

How did your preparation help you succeed?

Training in advance was key. I was able to keep working full-time while I went to school at night. I also did advance financial planning. Knowing that I was going to take a pay cut to quit Fannie Mae, I sold my old car early on and bought a car I knew would last a long time. I refinanced my apartment and got my mortgage payment down. Low expenses helped a lot.

What do you tell people who ask for your advice?

I tell them to ask themselves these three questions:

- What comes naturally to me?
- How do I love to spend my time?
- What makes me feel good about myself?

I tell them to contemplate those questions over and over again. It's tough. When you ask them how they love to spend their time, a lot of people say, "Well, I like to walk on the beach." Well, you can't make a living that way. You have to really sit with those questions. It's a process, and it may take years. Allow yourself to be open to exploring what comes up and then move in that direction, learn about it, and ultimately discover how to achieve it. It's important *not* to contemplate how in the beginning—it gets in the way, and creates obstacles. If you're passionate about something, you'll figure it out.

What books or resources did you use or recommend others to use?

Acupuncture books, of course. But mostly I made sure I was around only supportive people. I didn't want people asking questions like,

"Can you make a living doing that?" I wanted to move toward what I wanted to do and figure it out.

What are some of the surprises and unexpected rewards?

> "I began to look inside and answer some important questions: What am I best at? What are my gifts? Today, I know."

I never envisioned I'd go into fertility specialization. Now that is what I am known for. The workshops were a surprise as well. They evolved out of what I was doing with the fertility treatments, and now they are in such demand. I have been able to grow as a person by helping others with their process in those sessions.

Back to School

When you're looking to change careers as Lisa Eaves did, adding new skills is often a key to making a transition. But heading back for a full-blown master's degree is not really what most of us are looking for or need at this stage in our lives. It's pricey and a time zapper.

There are, however, some terrific certificate programs that can help you launch into a new field relatively quickly and for a fraction of the cost. Community colleges are a good place to start researching them. Many universities and trade groups and associations also offer programs that award certifications. You might also check the job boards for the positions that you are interested in pursuing and see what certifications are required for it.

The programs aren't always bargains, but when compared to an MBA, they can be. You can score a certificate in art appraisal, bookkeeping, chocolate making, eco-landscaping, fitness training, fundraising, home modification, and restaurant operations, to name a handful.

And employers and clients are gradually accepting professional certifications as confirmation of one's knowledge. That said, I recommend you research these programs with the eye of a potential employer, talk to students who are currently enrolled, and ask the program's director for details of where past grads are now working. Talk to employers about the value of the programs. Track a few down certificate holders and find out how the credential has helped them in their job search and new career path.

Most important, if you carve out the time and shell out for the coursework, you certainly want that certificate to have respect in the workplace.

When looking to become skilled in a new area, be sure to keep the following issues in mind:

Learn before you quit. If possible, keep your current job while you add the education you need for your new pursuit. Many employers offer tax-free tuition assistance programs—up to $5,250, not counted as taxable income—and the contribution doesn't have to be tagged to a full-degree program. You may have to repay the funds, though, if you don't stay with the company for a certain number of years afterward.

Seek financial aid. You don't need to be college age to get a subsidized loan—there's no age limit, and you're eligible as a part-time student, too. The federal aid formulas don't take into account your home equity or retirement accounts, and because you are an adult, a certain amount of your savings is protected—usually from $20,000 to $60,000, depending on your age and marital status. To apply for aid, complete the Free Application for Federal Student Aid (FAFSA) form.

Although it might be tempting to borrow from your home equity, you're better off with a low-interest Stafford loan (staffordloan.com). If you meet a financial needs test, the government will pay the interest as long as you're enrolled in school. The interest is currently a fixed rate of 5.41 percent. Rates are fixed for the life of the loan, but the rate for new loans will change annually. Many private lenders also offer loans, though rates will be higher.

Research scholarships and grants. These, too, are available for older students, usually offered by associations, colleges, religious groups, and foundations. Try sites such as Fastweb.com to find what's available.

Take advantage of educational tax breaks. Depending on your income, you might qualify for the lifetime learning credit, worth up to $2,000 each year. There's no limit to the number of years you can claim the credit. If you make too much, the income ceiling is higher for claiming a deduction associated with tuition and fees, up to $4,000. There's also a maximum student loan interest deduction of $2,500. For details, see the IRS website (irs.gov) or the tax benefits guide available from the National Association of Student Financial Aid Administrators (nasfaa.org).

TEN TIPS FOR PLANNING A WINNING SECOND CAREER

You might know you want to do something different but don't have the courage to do it yet. Take a breath. Lisa Eaves didn't decide one day that she wanted a new career as an acupuncturist and started the next day—she took her time and each step of the way reviewed whether she was following the right course for her personal gratification and researched the potential market.

1. **Understand what's behind your desire to make a change.** Maybe you are starting to become disillusioned with your work. You're bogged down. Perhaps you're no longer on the way up. This is the time to step back and begin to think about life more broadly. But be warned, career changers can go into mourning. All of a sudden, they realize what they could miss about their old career, and they're not really open to finding replacements.

   The longer time frame you have to plan, the better. Start working at age fifty on a career you might not get around to until age sixty. If you have lots of time, you can try out some ideas and possibilities, role-play, and do short stints at jobs that interest you to see if that is the direction you want to go.

2. **Get your life in order.** Get physically and financially fit. Change is stressful. When you're physically fit, you have more energy and are mentally sharper to face the challenges ahead. Starting a new career later in life takes an incredible amount of strength and energy. You need to be in good shape financially. Debt will kill your dreams. It limits your choices.

   A new career, too, is often a spiritual quest. You want to make a contribution or be connected with your inner desires and goals. Consider reading some of Deepak Chopra's books on spirituality and mind/body medicine. Check out my advice in Chapter 18, "Three-Part Fitness Program."

3. **Be practical.** If possible, make your move in stages. You may need to upgrade your skills and education, but take one class at a time. If you'd like to go to graduate school, maybe start by taking a night course. You don't have to enroll in a full course load. You can add more classes as your direction and motivation become clear.

   Overspending in your job search is another big mistake. Why shell out big bucks on advanced degrees, when a few courses will suffice? Why pay for a pricey résumé service before you've really thought through your next step? If possible, take some classes while your current employer is still offering tuition reimbursement (though be sure to investigate whether there is a payback requirement if you leave the firm). And check out gratis career services from your alma mater.

4. **Find a mentor.** Ask for help. Seek advice from people who have been successful in the field you want to enter. Everyone likes to be asked for counsel.

5. **Be prepared for setbacks.** It's not all smooth sailing, but if you've laid the proper groundwork, you'll get through the rough patches. Having your family or partner at your back for support will help tremendously. They don't have to own your dream but should be supportive.

6. **Volunteer or moonlight.** You might try on several jobs before you find the one that's right. Anne Nolan, president of Crossroads Rhode Island, the state's largest homeless shelter, started as a volunteer. (Read more in Chapter 5.) She didn't know what she wanted to do when she lost her executive-level job. She had a year's salary and time to think her options through. She decided to volunteer at the shelter—not because she dreamed it

would turn into a full-time job but because it was an activity that got her involved and took her mind away from worrying about what was next. It gradually became her passion. She was asked to join the board and then was hired on as the director. Look around you. Where might you lend a hand? Opportunity comes from the unexpected. Be open for it.

7. **Research.** Look for jobs that leverage experience. Check out job websites like Encore.org, RetiredBrains.com, RetirementJobs.com and Workforce50.com, to get a flavor for what others are doing and what jobs are out there now. Investigate fields like healthcare, the clergy, eldercare, and education that have a growing demand for workers. The Bureau of Labor Statistics' *Occupational Outlook Handbook* is a good reference.

8. **Don't lock yourself into a must-have salary.** Money is the biggest roadblock for most career changers. Chances are when you start over in a new field, you will need to take a salary cut at least initially. If you have an emergency fund to buy you time, you can to do a more thoughtful job search. Pare back your discretionary living expenses to reflect a more realistic view of what you'll earn. What are the things that are important in your life? What things are actively giving you pleasure that you might have to give up?

9. **Keep your hand out of the cookie jar.** Don't dip too deep into your core savings. Of all the mistakes older workers make in launching second careers, this is probably the single worst. Would-be entrepreneurs aren't necessarily raiding retirement accounts to launch businesses, but they're tapping home equity and other savings, and that has obvious implications for retirement security.

10. **Do something every day to work toward your goal.** Changing careers can seem overwhelming. "Don't struggle to find an ideal starting point or perfect path" is great advice I gleaned from Clearways Consulting career coach Beverly Jones, a second-acter herself. Once you have some picture of where you want to go, get things moving by taking small steps toward that vision. What really matters is that you do a little something on a regular basis.

Parting thought: A journey of a thousand miles starts with a single step, as the saying goes.

CHAPTER FOUR

A Kid Again Under the Big Top

When Donald Covington was a kid, he and his younger brother, Duncan, spent their summer days putting on backyard circuses at their Baltimore home. The devilish duo performed daring feats on bicycles and such, recruiting neighborhood kids to join in the fun.

Then each year, in late November, the Shrine Circus, produced by the Polack Bros. Circus, would set up shop in an old armory for a week, featuring top acts from all over the world. Covington would tag along with his father, who volunteered as an usher. "I remember sitting in the bleachers and hearing the echoing sounds of the animals, the people, and the band and the smells of cotton candy and popcorn. For me, it was the most exciting event of the year," he recalls.

Some things cling to you. After thirty years in the navy, Covington took mandatory retirement. And the navy captain, who once flew from the decks of carriers during the Vietnam War, ran away with the circus. The nonprofit, old-fashioned, one-ring Big Apple

Circus, to be precise, where he is the company manager for the 170-member traveling troupe and staff.

Covington lives on the road for forty-five weeks a year, shuttling from Boston to Atlanta with stops in ten cities or more. His trailer-home partner is the circus wardrobe supervisor—his wife, Janice—whom he met when she was a navy nurse. They have three grown children.

Retiring at age fifty, Covington could have worked for a defense contractor or flown for an airline. But the circus had never been far from his heart. Throughout his naval career, he attended circuses around the world and wrote reviews for *Circus Report*, a trade publication. So when he broached the idea of working for a circus, his family was supportive. "They knew the circus was important to me," Covington says, "and although no one shared my passion, they understood."

He talked to people he knew in the circus world, from Ringling Bros. to Big Apple. They gave him a feel for the pros and cons. And although he had no specific job in mind, he sent off his queries based on his military skill set—administration and management (he had commanded squadrons of 250 people or more), crisis management, the ability to react to unusual situations, and an understanding of a life of constant travel.

"When you think about it, the military and the circus are probably closer than most people would guess," Covington says. "It's a small group working very hard to achieve a goal. You have lots of specialists, and each is critical to what's going on. You also have the frustrations of life on the road and constantly adjusting to keep things going."

Big Apple's cofounders, Paul Binder and Michael Christensen, first hired him as a purchasing manager in charge of buying everything from feed for the horses to replacement tires for the trucks. And financially, with full retirement pay and benefits, he could afford to accept a job paying about half of his annual military salary. Climbing the ladder wasn't a concern, either. "The advantage to starting over in my situation was I had no pressing requirement to move up and become a director of something," Covington says. "I am very pleased to be a part of what goes on and do whatever I can to make things work, and that's a nice place to be."

On a stop at New York City's Lincoln Center, where the circus resides in mid-January, Covington's cramped office trailer sits adjacent to Big Apple's modest-size royal-blue big top. Inside, there's a forty-two-foot sawdust ring, surrounded by seventeen hundred seats, all within fifty feet of the action, creating an intimate setting for this classical circus.

"I can hear the music of the band," Covington says, "and walk over to watch the kids as they come into the tent and get the first look at the rigging, the seats, and the ring. At that moment, they simply say, 'Wow!' For me, that's heaven."

In a flash, he's ten years old again—and the circus is in town.

Author's Note: Don is now the president of the Circus Fans Association of America.

I asked Don to look back and share his thoughts on his transition to a career with the circus.

What did the transition mean to you personally?

I looked forward to it. I was very fortunate in that I came from something that I enjoyed—the navy—and landed at something

I also enjoy. Unlike people who take mandatory retirement and desperately need to find something to do, I went into a second career that has been as equally rewarding as the first. I look forward to coming to work every day. I like the people I work with, and I feel that what I do is important and is making a contribution.

Were you confident that you were doing the right thing? Any second-guessing?

I knew it was the right thing. There will always be surprises, but my lifestyle has been that way for as long as I can remember. The navy certainly taught me that there are going to be unexpected changes. That wasn't a big problem for me.

Anything you would have done differently?

If anything, I might have started a little bit sooner. I waited a little bit longer than I should have to do the research and make contacts or to look at possibilities. I was lucky that I found sympathetic ears when I talked to the people in the circus industry. They were eager to talk to me and very open about what I was getting into and what the options might be.

How do you measure your success?

It's coming to work every day and feeling good about what I am doing, enjoying what I do. I think that is most important for me. I feel like I am in the right place, and I am committed to what I am doing.

How big a role did financial rewards play in your decision to make a transition?

I had a retirement setup, so the move was not necessarily for the money. On the other hand, though, it is nice to still have a job and be able to continue to do the things we want to do. It means my wife and I are able to keep our home in San Diego, in addition to the RV we travel in. It also helps with paying off our kids' tuition bills.

How did your preparation make you succeed?

Again I was fortunate—the circus is something I have been interested in and passionate about my entire life, even before I ever considered it a second career. So I contacted everyone I knew who could offer advice and insight. I learned that the circus business is very forgiving to new people who pay their dues. It is up to you to learn the business, but the people are very supportive.

And my family was 100 percent behind my decision. My wife, Jan, has been quite supportive. We couldn't have done it otherwise. She understood the sacrifice that she would make because the circus is really my passion. She's a nurse. That's her profession. The circus is something she is doing so we can be together—and believe me, I really appreciate it!

What do you tell people who ask for your advice?

I tell them to make the effort to find something that fits them. It doesn't always have to be connected with good works or giving back to the community. Find something that makes sense for you, do it well, and do it 100 percent. If you can make that match, then everything else becomes worthwhile.

It's also important to start as soon as you can. If you know something that you want to do, talk to as many people as you can and do whatever research is appropriate, so that you'll feel comfortable when it is time to make the move.

> "The advantage to starting over in my situation was I had no pressing requirement to move up and become a director of something. I am very pleased to be a part of what goes on and do whatever I can to make things work, and that's a nice place to be."

What books or resources did you use or recommend others to use?

The navy has a transition program for those who are retiring. It was a great help to me and gave me perspective on the outside world, beyond the military. It covered financial planning, the psychology of how my transition would affect not only me but my family, too. It didn't give me the answers, but it helped give me the steps I needed to take.

What are some of the surprises and unexpected rewards?

I was concerned about our daughter, Anne, who was still in high school at the time, and how it would affect her. Now looking back on it—and I think she would agree with me—being on the road with the circus was a great place for her to grow up and go to school. She got a unique background, and it's helped her to be the person she is today.

On a deeper level, I didn't realize how proud it would make me feel. I never get tired of the circus. It's such a unique experience—the skills of the artists and the technical aspects of putting on a Broadway-quality show in a tent. I am part of the group that takes care of the details to be sure that things happen correctly, and I feel deeply proud of the result. I see it every day when people come and watch the show.

FIVE THINGS TO DO
BEFORE YOU LEAP TO A SECOND CAREER

1. **Check for help with career moves.** In the private sector, many U.S. corporations, small and large, are beginning to provide career coaches and counseling on a limited basis to help employees who have retired or lost their jobs. Increasingly, firms will put you in contact with career centers operated by area colleges or local government agencies offering workshops on résumé writing, career counseling, job fairs, and retraining programs.

2. **Do a background check.** This is your time to be inquisitive. Ask a lot of questions about the inner workings of an organization and what the work entails on a day-to-day basis. It's all about preparation. Knowing as much as you can is key to setting realistic expectations.

3. **Get your family on board.** If you have a family or partner, it's imperative that everyone understands the new

path you're embarking on and what it will entail. This might mean financial belt-tightening at first or increased travel.

You may find yourself working longer days than ever, too. So it's great if those closest to you don't make you feel guilty for your new regime.

4. **Don't let age get in your way.** When it comes to starting a new job, be forewarned: age discrimination is real. There's a perception that people over fifty or sixty will be just passing through as a transition into retirement. "Employers are loath to hire someone who they think will be out the door in a year or two," says Encore.org's Marc Freedman. But remember: It is *never* too late to start a second career. "The issue is not age but personal health, energy level, and an entrepreneurial spirit," Freedman says. "You need to be willing to prove that you still have what it takes."

5. **Feel positive about what you have to offer.** Workers over fifty tend to be self-starters, know how to get the job done, and don't need as much hand-holding as those with less experience. A great benefit to being older is that you have a great deal of accumulated knowledge. And whether you realize it or not, you have a network. You have a lot more resources to draw on than people in their twenties and thirties.

The Military as a Model

The military, a major employer in this country, really knows how to help its employees prepare for a second act. It's not unusual for military types like Don Convington to retire in their fifties with plenty of years left to segue into a new career in the civilian world. Little wonder that the Defense Department offers a transition jobs board with job postings from companies that hire veterans and their spouses.

Transition assistance programs help service members make the shift from soldier, sailor, air personnel, or marine to civilian as Covington did when he ran away with the circus. The programs, available at most installations, usually offer a two- or three-day class that covers the skills vital to finding a nonmilitary job, such as résumé writing, networking, interviewing, and job hunting. The Defense Department believes so strongly in this program that they've made it mandatory for all individuals who plan to leave the military or retire.

Many classes offer help with face-to-face job interviewing techniques and even how to dress for that meeting. Some provide sessions with private-sector business representatives who answer questions about opportunities in the job market and the skills that are essential for finding the best jobs. They hammer home ways for service members to sell their military experience, such as learning how to translate military jargon or acronyms that job interviewers might not be familiar with and how that skill might fit into their organization.

Transition counselors can purge some of that insider military speak into plain language to help bridge the gap between the two worlds. Other critical benefits of the military's transition program include job counseling for a spouse, relocation assistance services, help switching health insurance or other medical and dental coverage, counseling on the effects of career change on individuals and their families, and even financial planning assistance. While the military has been at the forefront of second career services, many corporations

are now offering free sessions with career counselors and job placement pros to employees who have been downsized, laid off, or accepted an early-retirement package. If you're not in the military, but
are offered such counseling or placement services by your company,
take full advantage of it, as this will assist you in transitioning to what's
next.

CHAPTER FIVE

At Home with the Homeless

When Anne Nolan first walked down the darkened steps into a homeless shelter, she started to cry. "I was so overwhelmed by the emotion of the place, the humanity, the pain," she recalls. "I was terrified and frightened. The dilapidated building was filthy, and it was mobbed with people lined up for food and shelter."

Today, Nolan is president of Crossroads Rhode Island, the state's largest provider of care and shelter to the homeless. The nonprofit now serves more than seventy-five hundred people, from a newborn to an eighty-nine-year-old, and demand is growing. "When our consumer base grows, that's not a good thing," Nolan notes. "And we're busting at the seams."

Spoken like the veteran of corporate America that Nolan is. Her career path includes stints as a university professor (she has a master's in counseling and a doctorate in education) and nearly thirty years working for big companies like Fleet Financial Group and Digital Equipment in various senior executive slots.

But her everyday world was . . . flat. "There was no passion," Nolan says. Big salaries and year-end bonuses had kept her tied to those corporate posts. "I got so far away from where my heart had been back in my idealist days growing up in the sixties. I had started my career in education with such energy and enthusiasm and a belief that I could make a difference." At fifty-two, she was years from retirement. But when her company dissolved, she had the chance to step off the corporate merry-go-round, with a year's pay to tide her over.

She started to walk with her dog six or seven miles a day along the Blackstone River, which allowed her to do some soul-searching. "I wanted to do something that would make me proud, something to feel passionate about. Something that would make me cry for the good reasons," she says. And one day, something shifted. "'That's it,' I said out loud. 'I'm not going back to the corporate world. I'm going to work for a not-for-profit.'" Nolan heard about Travelers Aid, the old name for Crossroads, arranged to meet with the president, and paid her first visit to a shelter. "I knew I had found my place," she says. Whenever Nolan bought a lottery ticket and dreamed of what she would do if she won, it was always the same fantasy: start a nonprofit to help homeless families. A strange choice, she says, considering that her only exposure to homeless people was stepping around them on city streets.

Impressed with Nolan's corporate background, the president named her to a board position that first day. Later, when the president left, Nolan got the job. The pay: only about half her six-figure corporate compensation. She did belt-tightening and tapped into her home equity—all worth it, she says. "I love my job. You can't put a price on that."

It turns out that her corporate career had readied her to help the homeless. "I held a patchwork of unrelated positions and industries that suddenly all connected. Whether it was financial controls or organizational development, environmental construction or an FDIC audit—suddenly it was all relevant."

Nolan used her business acumen to transform Crossroads Rhode Island into more than just a shelter and soup kitchen. Yes, food and shelter are available 24/7, but there is also a range of housing options, full-spectrum healthcare and dental service, basic adult literacy and GED training, and job search help. There's a nursing assistant training program and even hands-on instruction in printing and graphics.

Crossroads has helped well over thirty-three thousand adults and children over the past ten years. The nonprofit's annual budget is now more than $11 million, up from some $3 million when Nolan started, as the number of donors has grown nearly tenfold. She says she has even bigger dreams for Crossroads. Nolan still cries sometimes when she enters the shelter, but it's no longer from despair.

I asked Anne to look back and share her thoughts on her transition to running a homeless shelter.

What did the transition mean to you personally?

I hate to sound corny, but I felt like a weight was lifted from me. My corporate career had lost its focus and meaning, and over the years, it just got heavier and heavier. I didn't even realize how much it had been weighing me down. I also gained an incredible sense of appreciation for my own life. I don't think a day has gone by that I haven't felt grateful for the little things. I think I lost that in my corporate career.

Were you confident that you were doing the right thing? Any second-guessing?

I never second-guessed my decision. And that was interesting because I got a lot of discouraging remarks. People told me I had no business thinking I could all of a sudden decide to work for a nonprofit, because I didn't have any experience. A nonprofit recruiter actually told me I should stay in corporate and just make donations! She was really rude. She basically said, "Who do you think you are? People have been working for thirty years in the nonprofit world and you just want to parachute in."

But I just knew. In this case, it was just so clear to me. I thought, no, you're wrong. I know where I belong.

Anything you would have done differently?

I'm not sure there was anything I could have done differently.

How do you measure your success?

It's the fact that when Sunday night comes around, I have no dread. I look forward to Monday morning. And as long as I can look forward to Monday morning, I know I am doing the right thing.

How big a role did financial rewards play in your decision to make a transition?

None whatsoever. In fact, I remortgaged my house once again, and it has been worth every ounce of debt I incurred.

How did your preparation help you succeed?

It is very cliché, but I followed what the books say. I got out there. I networked. I met as many people as I could. I did this spiderweb of contacts and networking. And I had volunteered beforehand.

Once I made the decision that I wanted to work for a nonprofit, and this one in particular, I joined the board. I was asked to, which was great. I just followed their rules of how to get the job.

There is no magic. All of my skills from my corporate experience translated, and that was an important piece of the puzzle. It is very clear to me that the profit and nonprofit worlds are merging—as more and more things like compliance, regulations, and scrutiny are now applied to the nonprofit world. I was able to use the right language, and I think it has been to Crossroads's advantage that I have that corporate background.

And my skills were not the only thing I felt prepared me. I was also realistic about my weaknesses. There were things I knew nothing about, and I knew when to get help.

What do you tell people who ask for your advice?

You have to know what you want to do. That's the hard part—really feeling right about your decision. I always tell people to take their time. When I was making my own decisions, I walked all the time with my dog. Everybody has a different way of processing. They have to find what that is and take the time to really understand their options and not do anything rash. I advise people to spend time with this kind of self-exploration, until they know.

> "I wanted to do something that would make me proud, something to feel passionate about. Something that would make me cry for the good reasons."

What books or resources did you use or recommend others to use?

Well, there is the old classic *What Color Is Your Parachute?* I read it years and years ago.

What are some of the surprises and unexpected rewards?

I didn't expect it to be as much fun—but I have fun every day. We laugh hysterically here. I love the people I work with, both the clients and staff. I also didn't expect the diversity of the job. One minute I'm in Washington talking to senators, and the next minute I'm with a family in need. It is just amazing to me.

REASON TO VOLUNTEER

There's no question that giving back feels good, but it can also offer a sense of whether a certain career field truly inspires you. This was true for Anne Nolan and could be true for you, too.

Volunteering also keeps existing professional skills up-to-date. According to the Bureau of Labor Statistics, about 64.3 million people volunteered for an organization in 2011. "Individuals with higher levels of educational attainment engaged in volunteer activities at higher rates than did those with less education," the report found. To break it down, a whopping 42.4 percent of all volunteers held a bachelor's degree or higher. So your chances of meeting professionals in the volunteer pool are promising.

Moreover, as I write in my book *Great Jobs for Everyone 50+: Finding Work That Keeps You Happy and Healthy . . . and Pays the Bills*, volunteer experience can grab a potential employer's interest. Many companies look favorably on people who are socially responsible. Do-gooders are valued. And volunteering can show your openness to learning new things, coming up with creative ways to do things for less and provide hands-on guidance when a nonprofit is understaffed or lacks resources.

In fact, 41 percent of the two thousand professionals that LinkedIn surveyed said that when they appraise candidates, they consider volunteer work as valuable as paid work experience. If you already have a history of volunteering, list the specific charity or business and the dates you worked on your résumé and LinkedIn profile. I suggest that you don't use the word *volunteer* as your title. Choose a more specific descriptor, such as *fundraiser* or *project manager.* Be sure to underscore what your volunteer work helped the organization achieve—for example, results, returns, special awards, or honors you personally received for your pro bono work. Of course, in the job description, you should state that it was a volunteer project. This stresses your philanthropy, but by defining it as a professional job, you give it credibility.

Ultimately, volunteering bolsters your résumé with a new facet and reflects on your character in a positive fashion.

You might also consider seeking out intern, shadowing, or volunteer opportunities at for-profit firms. Make an appointment with the hiring manager or owner of a business and meet in person to pose the question of whether he or she would be willing to show you the ropes in exchange for your free labor. If it's a small business, say, a neighborhood bistro, introduce yourself to the owner and explain what you're looking for and what hours you're free to work.

Suggest a trial work plan, perhaps a couple of hours a day for a week or two, so the owner won't feel bogged down with an obligation to you. Be open to doing the dirty work. Make it your goal to work hard, ask lots of questions and see where the job leads.

Volunteering is a genuine path to a full-time job. An employer gets a chance to check you out and vice versa. It can be a great test trial for both of you. Even if the particular employer doesn't work out, you're still able to get an understanding of that type of work and an overall feel for the industry. You might find it wasn't what you dreamed it would be. But that's worth knowing before you get too far down the road to your dream job.

That said, you may love the business, make new friends, and even connect with a possible mentor who can help you get your feet on the ground, act as a sounding board, and introduce you to others in the field.

Where to Find Volunteer Projects

Myriad online services can connect you with both short-term and long-term volunteer projects and potential nonprofit jobs that match your interests.

- HandsOn Connect (1-800-volunteer.org) provides a database of more than twenty-six thousand projects nationwide and allows you to search by county.

- Ashoka (ashoka.org) supports the work of social entrepreneurs. Volunteers are needed to translate documents and assist with fundraising, marketing, website design, research, writing, graphic design, and technical support.

- BoardnetUSA (boardnetusa.org) places people on the boards of nonprofits. You fill out a profile of your interests and professional skills; nonprofits then choose whether to interview you for their board positions.

- The Bridgespan Group (bridgespan.org) runs the online Nonprofit Jobs Center, which now has about 330 positions, including paid part-time and full-time jobs and volunteer options.

- Commongood Careers (cgcareers.org) is a headhunter for nonprofits looking to hire management-level types. Click the "Find a Job" tab on their website to apply directly for openings with their clients. You might also find volunteer board opportunities.

- Create the Good (createthegood.com) is an AARP website that lets you find good works to do in your community and posts volunteer opportunities. How-to videos can help you start your own volunteer project.

- Doctors Without Borders/Médecins Sans Frontières (MSF) (doctorswithoutborders.org) is an international medical humanitarian organization created by doctors and journalists in France in 1971. Today, MSF provides aid in nearly sixty countries to people whose survival is threatened by violence, neglect, or catastrophe, primarily due to armed conflict, epidemics, malnutrition, exclusion from healthcare, or natural disasters.

- The Foundation Center (foundationcenter.org) is a premier site that is chock-a-block with philanthropy information and news. Sign up for the "Philanthropy News Digest" newsletter to learn about opportunities at foundations and nonprofits. Recently, there were 722 listings in the database.

- HandsOn Network (handsonnetwork.org), the volunteer-activation arm of Points of Light, features skills-based volunteer opportunities. The network includes 250 community action centers that deliver thirty million hours of volunteer service each year in sixteen countries around the world. These centers focus on helping people plug into volunteer opportunities in their local communities, partnering with more than seventy thousand corporate, faith, and nonprofit organizations to manage volunteer resources, and developing the leadership capacity of volunteers.

- Idealist (idealist.org) offers leads to more than fourteen thousand volunteer opportunities nationwide, plus internships and jobs in the nonprofit sector. It also offers an extensive jobs board with more than ten thousand jobs currently posted. You can search by job function, such as fundraising, marketing, and accounting. You can also drill down to sort for part-time, full-time, or contract work and even salary or education requirements.

- Lawyers Without Borders (lawyerswithoutborders.org) directs legal pro bono services and resources to human rights initiatives, legal capacity-building projects, and rule-of-law projects around the world. It seeks volunteers with a legal background—practicing or retired lawyers, law students, and others who have worked as legal support staff—to manage projects and sustain home and branch office operations. Volunteer tasks can include newsletter editing and layout, grant writing, graphic design, program development, and management.

- *The NonProfit Times* (thenonprofittimes.com/jobs) is the trade publication for nonprofit managers. Its website houses the Non-Profit Jobs Career Center, where you can search for positions by keyword, field, location, salary, and required education.

- Operation Hope (operationhope.org) seeks individuals with a background in the financial industry (mortgage brokers, bankers, tax consultants, etc.) to work as virtual volunteers, from any location with Internet access. Volunteers provide ongoing case management to victims of hurricanes and other disasters and offer financial and budget counseling over the phone. Those who want to be involved receive training and software and can work from their home or office.

- The Retired Senior Volunteer Program (RSVP) division of Senior Corps (seniorcorps.org), a program of the Corporation for National and Community Service, matches people fifty-five years or older with volunteer opportunities. The programs are typically sponsored locally by area nonprofits, and some offer compensation or a small stipend. Most of the programs provide health insurance for the volunteers.

- United We Serve (serve.gov) is a national online resource not only for finding volunteer opportunities in your community but also for creating your own. It's managed by the Corporation for National and Community Service.

- The Taproot Foundation (taprootfoundation.org) organizes teams of highly skilled volunteer professionals to provide consulting to local nonprofits. Assignments are based on the volunteer's professional experience in a variety of fields, including finance, marketing, and information technology. Taproot, which is active in seven U.S. cities, sets up teams of five professionals who commit to at least five hours a week, for five months.

- America's Natural and Cultural Resources Volunteer Portal (volunteer.gov) is a one-stop shop for public service volunteer projects sponsored by the U.S. government.

- VolunteerMatch (volunteermatch.org) allows you to search more than seventy-three thousand listings nationwide. Its extensive database of projects lets you screen for everything from board opportunities to communications positions based on your interests and geographical location.

Opportunities with Pay

Some short-term nonprofit work options come with a paycheck. You may be able to land a paid internship or fellowship that lets your dip your toe into the nonprofit world to see if it suits you and potentially sync up with a future full-time employer.

Coming of Age (comingofage.org) is a Philadelphia-based outfit that helps people fifty years and older explore their future and connect and contribute to their communities through paid and unpaid opportunities. They provide training to nonprofits about how to build their capacity to capture the energy and expertise of this growing segment of the population. Coming of Age has expanded to other areas around the country, so check for a group near you.

Encore Fellows are paired with nonprofits, where they typically commit to a thousand hours over a six- to twelve-month period, working part- or full-time. The fellowships come with a $25,000 stipend. The number of available fellowships is limited and the application and selection process is competitive. To learn more, visit their website (encore.org/fellowships) or send an email to info@encorefel lowships.net.

The **Rose Community Foundation** (rcfdenver.org) is a Denver-based organization that trains older adults to become navigators or community health workers.

ReServe (reserveinc.org) is a nonprofit agency that connects professionals over fifty-five years with experience in marketing, accounting, and other areas with more than 350 government agencies and nonprofit groups in the New York City area, Boston, Newark, Baltimore, Southeast Wisconsin, and Miami to part-time projects that offer a modest stipend (such as $10 an hour). Individuals can expect to work fifteen to twenty hours a week. Current Reservists can check out the online Opportunities board, which lists openings.

CHAPTER SIX

A Lawyer Does Business with New Partners

Sam Fox is not a gentleman farmer. But by all rights, the once high-powered patent attorney could be.

Maybe even a city slicker to boot. Fox spent nearly his entire life in Washington, DC, before retiring as managing partner from Sterne, Kessler, Goldstein & Fox, an intellectual-property law firm.

Today, Fox raises purebred Polled Hereford cattle and harvests hay at his 187-acre spread outside Sperryville, Virginia, in the shadow of the Shenandoah Mountains. His crew of farmhands consists of his wife, Elizabeth, and two yellow Labrador retrievers.

His hours are long, maybe even longer than those seven-day weeks he spent working in the law firm's early days. Now he starts at first light and runs into the wee hours during calving season.

In 1988, Fox acquired the run-down, termite-infested stable and rolling land as an investment. He bought it the day he saw it. "Visually, it was just extraordinary," he says. Very quickly, he became "totally smitten with the countryside, the people, and the way of life. Pretty soon, I was looking for something that would allow me to be here and have something to do as well."

He succeeded. It began with a rebuilding of the courtyard-style stable, square foot by square foot, into a home. It evolved into a farming business in 1998, when he purchased four pregnant cows from a neighbor. "I had been spending a lot of money on this place, doing everything from the building to the fencing, and I thought there could be a way to turn this into a business," he says.

Knowing that Fox was in the country only on weekends, the same neighbor volunteered to keep the cows for him. He also became Fox's mentor on the ways of cattle farming and haymaking. Other neighbors have pitched in, too, to help him find his way in the country. "They know I am trying," he says, "and they don't think less of me because I don't know something."

Fox started by visiting the property every Sunday. Progress was slow. First, electricity was added, and next a well was drilled for running water. Then he logged the one-hour, forty-minute trip from Washington for the entire weekend. Before he knew it, he was devoting every spare minute to the farm. "Instead of taking vacations at the beach, I came here," he says. In time, Fox realized that he wanted to be able to work the farm and do it full-time while he was still relatively young.

The learning curve has been steep. "I lost a calf the other day because I didn't realize the heifer was in trouble. Next time, I'll know," he says.

And the carpentry needed to make the place livable was far more than he had imagined. "If I had known the extent of the work the place needed, I never would have undertaken it," he says. "I wasn't born for this. I didn't work in the building trades. As I made my way around the building, stud by stud, I thought, at any minute, this whole thing is going to come down."

But the intrinsic rewards are many for this city boy: "I feel like I have built something really beautiful, and that's very satisfying to me. I'm proud of it." For Fox, it's proof that "you can make anything happen as long as you are willing to work at it."

He now owns thirty-two cows, five heifers, one steer, and two bulls. This spring, thirty calves were born, most of which will be sold at auction. About half of the land is in pasture or hay production, the balance wooded.

While the farming business is not generating big profits, the operation doesn't need to do so. The Foxes' retirement savings are enough to cover their living expenses.

Fox is toying with trying to develop a market where he could sell directly to the consumer, and he could raise his cattle entirely on grass and organically. For now, though, it remains a calf/cow operation, which sells off the calves to a middleman, long before they're sold for meat. Fox revels in the challenging process of breeding quality cows and raising young calves—even those that require bottle-feeding by hand, as two who lost their mothers did this past spring.

"I never loved being a lawyer," Fox says. "I enjoyed managing the firm and loved the people there. But the farm is my real passion." He doesn't actually see himself as the owner, but rather, the steward of the property—looking after it for the next people who come through.

I asked Sam to look back and share his thoughts on his transition to farming.

What did the transition mean to you personally?

I reacted so emotionally to this land, this terrain. I was really looking forward to being here. I wanted to live here. I never loved practicing law. I wanted a different life, living in the country, working outside—I can honestly say I had very few regrets about leaving the law firm. I miss the people, but I didn't miss the type of stress that I had. I feel bound to this place. I have a greater feeling and sense of responsibility for the animals than I ever thought I would.

Were you confident that you were doing the right thing? Any second-guessing?

I never second-guessed.

Anything you would have done differently?

I would have done it thirty years earlier!

How do you measure your success?

There are many levels to it: How am I caring for the land? Am I doing a good job? Have I improved the immediate environment? Am I treating my cattle appropriately?

When I practiced law, I had lots of anxious moments, and they all revolved around money. Now I am dealing with the lives of animals. It is a completely different level of responsibility. There are nights when I can't sleep because a calf's just been born, and it's cold out. Is it all right? Should I go out at midnight? At 2 a.m.?

There's still a lot of anxiety for me, but seeing a healthy calf at its mother's side is the greatest reward.

How did your preparation help you succeed?

I was able to gradually prepare myself and get involved little by little. The first ten years I was here, I just worked on the building itself. During that time, I enrolled in a range of classes on farming. While I was still a lawyer, I took courses in cow/calf management at the University of Virginia, for example. They offered class work on various topics, including health, birthing issues, and things of that nature. It taught me the real nuts and bolts of how to run a successful operation from a business as well as an agricultural and veterinary perspective.

My previous life experience played a big role, too. Before practicing law, I had a business in the chemical industry, and I learned to do electrical and plumbing work. I have always been interested in woodworking and had basic carpentry skills. I was also interested in mechanics, which helped when it came to maintaining all the farm equipment. Because of those previous interests, I was better prepared to come out and live and work on the land.

Ultimately, I was never afraid to ask questions. I have no pride about that. I continue to learn all the time.

What do you tell people who ask your advice?

Most people think I'm crazy! Rarely does anyone ask me for advice. But if they did, I'd tell them that retiring is not an easy thing to do. I know people who flunked retirement. They don't know what to do with themselves.

What was different for me was that I had a true passion about what I wanted to do. I felt directed toward this life. I did stay on [as a lawyer] part-time for a couple more years, so I didn't leave the firm high and dry.

The other thing that made it possible was that my life partner was fully supportive. Elizabeth never ever said, "Hey, this is a bad idea" or "Are you sure you want to do this?" She knew it was what I wanted to do, and she has always loved it out here, too.

Elizabeth is fully involved in the farming operation. She is very intuitive. Having her help and support has been key to making this change. There are plenty of times when I don't know what I'm doing, and we'll talk it over—having Elizabeth with me makes a huge difference.

What books or resources did you use or recommend others to use?

The Merck Veterinary Manual.

What are some of the surprises and unexpected rewards?

I have always felt a little bit like an outsider no matter what I've done. I started practicing law later in life, and I never really felt like a lawyer. I moved to the farm and never exactly felt I was a farmer. And there are certain people here who resent outsiders. But there are people who've made me feel appreciated because they realized what my level of commitment was. They could see that. And I've been pleasantly surprised by the acceptance that I have received from certain portions of the community.

> "I feel like I have built something really beautiful, and that's very satisfying to me. I'm proud of it. You can make anything happen as long as you are willing to work at it."

I realize now that I *am* a farmer. That's what I do. I'm not a lawyer out here fiddling around. I'm not a lawyer at all, anymore.

We're farming. That's what we're doing. There's no way to make any money, but it's the grandest life you could ever hope for. I'm not a city boy anymore. I don't think of myself as someone who comes here on weekends. This is my home. This is all there is for me.

SLOW AND STEADY

A successful career change is a process. So be patient. It might even take a few years to lay all the groundwork you will need to begin again. Here are the four golden rules to follow.

1. *Talk to people.* Find people who are currently doing the work you want to be doing, and seek their advice and

counsel. Take the time to nurture these relationships. You may find them in unlikely places—from the local hardware store to a conference—so be open to a variety of sources.

2. *Upgrade your skills and education.* Chances are you'll need to bone up on new skills and maybe even earn another degree. If possible, take required courses *before* you quit your current job. Professional programs, grad schools, and community colleges offer evening and weekend classes that you can fit into your existing schedule without having to make a major move. Your current employer might even foot the bill, but make sure you check the fine print—you might have to repay tuition expenses if you leave your job within a certain time frame.

3. *Start small and give yourself time to grow and learn.* If possible, start your new venture with baby steps and let it evolve. Making a change in stages allows you to work at something you are passionate about without taking a wild leap. In time, you may be able to grow a hobby into a profitable enterprise.

4. *Don't be afraid to ask questions.* Bury your pride or fear of sounding stupid or naive. It never hurts to ask others for help. Being a newcomer is always uncomfortable, particularly if you were in a position of authority in your old line of work. If you want to learn, you have to be willing to set all that aside and simply admit you don't know something. You're sure to find plenty of others who have asked those same questions along the way and will be more than happy to pass on the favor.

What Is a Social Entrepreneur?

According to Ashoka (ashoka.org)—the largest network of social entrepreneurs worldwide, with nearly three thousand Ashoka Fellows in seventy countries putting their system-changing ideas into practice on a global scale—social entrepreneurs are individuals with innovative solutions to society's most pressing social problems. They are ambitious and persistent, tackling major social issues, such as economic opportunities for women in the Middle East, North Africa, Turkey, and Pakistan, and finding ways to allay serious youth violence, adolescent antisocial behavior, and crime in the United Kingdom.

Rather than leaving societal needs to the government or business sectors, social entrepreneurs find what is not working and solve the problem by changing the system, spreading the solution, and persuading entire societies to take new leaps.

Social entrepreneurs often seem to be possessed by their ideas, committing their lives to changing the direction of their field. They are both visionaries and ultimate realists, concerned with the practical implementation of their vision above all else.

Each social entrepreneur presents ideas that are user friendly, understandable, and ethical and engage widespread support to maximize the number of local people who will stand up, seize their idea, and implement it. In other words, every leading social entrepreneur is a mass recruiter of local change makers—a role model proving that citizens who channel their passion into action can do almost anything.

Just as entrepreneurs change the face of business, social entrepreneurs act as the change agents for society, seizing opportunities others miss and improving systems, inventing new approaches, and creating solutions to change society for the better. While a business entrepreneur might create entirely new industries, a social entrepreneur comes up with new solutions to social problems and then implements them on a large scale.

Organizations That Support Social Entrepreneurs

While Sam Fox is not looking to change the world with a mission of selling beef with a social purpose, his humane approach to farming is akin to others who are pursuing second-career work with meaning through start-up ventures that serve the homeless, the hungry, and the environment. If you are heading in this direction and have the social entrepreneurial spirit, here are some leading organizations that can help you get going:

- Ashoka (ashoka.org) has elected over two thousand leading social entrepreneurs as Ashoka Fellows, providing them with living stipends, professional support, and access to a global network of peers in more than seventy countries.

- Echoing Green (echoinggreen.org) supports social entrepreneurs in launching new organizations. It offers a two-year fellowship program to help entrepreneurs develop new solutions to society's most difficult problems. Typically less than 1 percent of their thousands of applicants are ultimately selected to receive financial support.

- Encore.org (encore.org) is a San Francisco–based nonprofit dedicated to advancing social entrepreneurship and work with meaning.

- GlobalGiving (globalgiving.com) enables individuals and companies to find and support social and economic development projects around the world.

- The Investors' Circle Network (investorscircle.net) is made up of angel investors, professional venture capitalists, foundations, family offices, and others who are using private capital to promote the transition to a sustainable economy. Since 1992 the Investors' Circle has facilitated the flow of over $172 million into more than 270 companies and small funds addressing social and environmental issues. Members tend to invest in the following categories: environment, education, health, and community.

- The Schwab Foundation for Social Entrepreneurship (schwab found.org) works with Harvard University, Stanford University, and INSEAD to provide scholarship opportunities to the best executive education courses in the field to selected social entrepreneurs.

- The Skoll Foundation's (skollfoundation.org) mission is to advance systemic change to benefit communities around the world by investing in, connecting, and celebrating social entrepreneurs. The foundation extends its mission through Social Edge, an online resource for the social entrepreneur community.

CHAPTER SEVEN

Where Work Really Is a Zoo

Howard Baskin admits that a few homeless cats have won his heart over the years, but saving abandoned and abused lions, lynxes, and leopards was by no means his dream, let alone his passion. When it came to giving to animal causes, he might write a modest check to the Humane Society of the United States. His world was finance and marketing. Yet there's no denying that a stroll where he works at the forty-five-acre Big Cat Rescue—a nonprofit educational sanctuary in Tampa, one of the largest in the world devoted to the big cats—leaves him inspired.

This is where Bengal tigers, African lions, snow leopards, bobcats, and other exotic cats recline gracefully on tree limbs, stretch languidly in their dens, or splash playfully in ponds amid shady oaks and palmettos. In all, there are over one hundred feline residents with permanent homes here. "Looking at these animals and realizing that I've been able to make a difference in the quality of their lives and securing their future is wonderful," he says.

Baskin isn't one of the cats' caregivers, but he uses his financial acumen to ensure they live a healthful life. With a Harvard MBA and a law degree, he spent the first eleven years of his career at Citicorp, rising to become director of strategic planning for the commercial real-estate division in New York. "Working in a small business had always been my plan, but I kept getting interesting jobs at the bank," he recalls.

He left Citi to work as a management consultant for a succession of small companies. Eight years later, he opted for a less stressful pace, consulting part time and freeing up time for tennis and leisurely rounds of golf. But something was missing.

And in 2003, just a few years into his semiretired bachelor life, he did an about-face. Before he knew it, he had ramped up to sixty-hour workweeks at the sanctuary and agreed to take charge of its finances for free. Sure, Baskin is fond of the cats, but it was another love that inspired him. His wife, Carole, whom he met in 2002 and married in 2004, founded the twenty-one-year-old sanctuary and is CEO.

"I kind of married into this transition, although it was, of course, my choice, not a requirement," Baskin says. "I fell in love with her. One thing that drew me to her was her passion for the mission and the excitement of working for a cause, not just a living."

Take Nikita, for example. The lioness spent her first year living on a concrete slab, chained to a wall by a drug dealer in Nashville. She was discovered in a raid and arrived at Big Cat with sores on her elbows the size of tennis balls.

Not all of the cats were abused, though. Some were abandoned by owners who could no longer afford to care for them. Others were retired from circus acts, rescued from fur farms, or obtained from roadside zoos that had fallen on hard times.

Baskin came well prepared to bolster the sanctuary's shaky financial underpinnings. The small firms where he used to work ran the gamut from a bridge builder to a foundry to an audiovisual firm. They were businesses whose finances were in disarray when he arrived. Someone had to figure out how to get things organized and create systematic controls.

And he has. Donations of $1.2 million to Big Cat in 2012 were ten times the amount raised in 2003. And Carole now has time to advocate for laws to crack down on illegal animal dealers and implement humane care standards for the cats.

Although Baskin would like to spend a bit more time on the golf course, there's little other downside. His full-time consulting income, which at one time topped six figures, had already been trimmed, and he had a thrifty lifestyle, plenty of savings, and growing retirement funds.

Today his salary is under $50,000 annually. "But I get a double payback. Not only do I get to do something for the cats," he says as he watches Nikita devour her afternoon "bloodsicle" snack, "but I feel like I am contributing to the world. More important, I get to make Carole happy. That's my number one goal."

I asked Howard to look back and share his thoughts on his transition to a career with the nonprofit Big Cat with me.

What did the transition mean to you personally?

It's a little odd because this is really my third act. When I left banking and decided I wanted to go into my own business, that was a conscious, planned decision. I kind of just fell into this. There wasn't that element of thinking through what I wanted to do.

In fact, this wasn't even something that would have been on the radar. I've enjoyed animals. I've had pets, but I never thought of myself as getting passionately involved with animals. I stumbled on it. If there is any lesson to come from it, it is to be open to things that you don't think of that come your way serendipitously. There are no coincidences.

Were you confident that you were doing the right thing? Any second-guessing?

I was completely confident. The reason for that probably was what I found at the sanctuary was not all that different from what I knew from the small businesses I had gone into before. The marketing and finance aspects, for example, and so I had done that enough that I could look at it and say, "OK, here's where we are, here's where we have to get, and here's how we do that."

The part that was a mystery to me that I was much less confident about, and really had to learn by trial and error, was fundraising. Even obvious things were not obvious for me. I had a small list of causes that I donated to myself, among which were environmental causes, but my giving wasn't focused on animals. I didn't even have the experience of being a particularly active donor.

I had to learn what makes someone donate money and get really involved in a cause. And so that's where I tried picking up things to read and looked at what other people were doing. There are simple things I learned, such as how you recognize donors physically on the property. I didn't know anything about that need to physically and visibly thank donors for their kindness. I would go to the other venues and see how they created signs to honor people who had contributed.

In the early years . . . park benches, for example; I asked myself, what would [people] pay to put their names on them—let me try $250. And the twenty-five benches sold out. At that time we had very few $250 donations. A $100 donation was a big deal then. Now we have many more $500 donors . . . and $1,000 donors. . . . That was a very rare occurrence. It almost sounds silly because it is so obvious, but there was this real aha! People who wouldn't otherwise donate will donate if they get their name on something. I'm still learning. In 2012, we had nineteen donors of $5,000 and above.

Anything you would have done differently?

The one part of this that I did not anticipate was just how much hard work it was going to be. I had made a conscious decision after working long hours during my school life and through my career to cut back, and I was really enjoying that. Not just in a frivolous way from the fact that there was leisure time, but I was also enjoying the lack of pressure and the lack time pressure and the stress they create.

When I think back, I could have limited my role. I could have said, "Look I am going to do the financial record keeping of this and not worry about the donation side." I probably would have had a lot less stress the last few years. But we wouldn't be where we are today. So I wouldn't have that satisfaction.

As donations grew I couldn't handle it back in 2006. . . . Now I have come to the point where I'm almost sixty-five, and I just don't want to have this kind of stress until I am eighty, so I have been working on a plan to cut back. I hired one of our volunteers to be a director of donor appreciation. I feel confident to pass on the duties. Very selfishly, I hope it will allow me to cut back to a more normal balance of life.

How do you measure your success?

I'll divide that question into two. As far as success for the endeavor, I'm very proud of our gaining financial footing. There are metrics like the number of visitors and the number of donations.

When it comes to the psychic success related specifically to the mission, seeing some of these cats come in from these horrible places, fearful and stressed out, and in time, they become happy, playful, and content, and we see them physically fill out, that is an immeasurable feeling. That transformation is extremely rewarding.

Keep in mind, a tiger is a $10,000-a-year commitment, and that's just food and medicine, no overhead. The number is more than double that when you allocate the entire overhead, and people can't keep it up, so the animals wind up neglected and in very bad shape by the time they come to us.

How big a role did financial rewards play in your decision to make a transition?

In fact, it was very much the opposite. In the years that I have been here, my net worth has not grown at all. Ideally, these would be the years when you would like to be building for retirement.

How did your preparation help you succeed?

My past jobs helped. I was able to apply for-profit principles to a nonprofit. And any chance I got to corner someone who had experience in this area, I would grab a lunch with him or her, anything that I could to do to tap the other person's brain. I started going to meetings with nonprofit people. I didn't take courses, but there were some seminars that I went to. There's one organization for chief executives of nonprofits, and I went to some for their classes. That was quite helpful.

What do you tell people who ask for your advice?

I have a number of people who use me as a sounding board and an adviser both personally and career. One suggestion I have is to be open to nonprofit work as one of the options. The rewards of what you can accomplish in the nonprofit world, the psychic rewards, are something that it's hard to contemplate or really appreciate until you have experienced something like that. It seems obvious to say it, but it will be rewarding, and the intensity of that reward is something that is hard to forecast or fully understand or foresee until you have done it.

Once you make the decision go for it. Run with it as hard as you can. And if it's not the direction you want to keep going at some point, then make another decision, but don't go back and say I would have been much better off with the other decision because you just don't know that.

What are some of the surprises and unexpected rewards?

Besides the fact that Carole still says she is the happiest woman in the world and I am to blame for that, it's the people in the community I have met.

In my past jobs, I never had to do the kind of networking I have had to here. I joined the local Rotary. I was on the board of the Upper Tampa Bay Chamber of Commerce. While these were time burdensome, they built relationships that paid off in an array of ways—from a financial standpoint, a business community standpoint, and a personal one.

My involvement with those groups built credibility in the early years. It has also been personally very rewarding to build the friendships with a very remarkable bunch of people. If you are in the Rotary, for instance, you have made a decision to do some giving back to the community.

You're meeting people who are generally successful and interesting and have an element of their psyche that is oriented toward community service. The other area that I didn't think about at all is the joy of dealing with the donors, who are really passionate about what we do. It is very satisfying and enjoyable and some of these people have become real friends. It feels good. I take personal pleasure when they compliment me on what we are accomplishing and doing.

And I am so proud that Carole has made us a recognized leader in social media. Our YouTube channel, BigCatTV.com, has had more than *sixty million* views and has been a huge part of building our awareness. We're close to a hundred thousand Facebook fans now.

Finally, and very important, we have become the national leader in the fight to stop abuse of captive big cats.

Ways to Prepare for Nonprofit Work

If you choose to go the nonprofit route by switching to a job in the nonprofit sector, you will need to be ready for different scenes than the for-profit world you may be accustomed to.

- Don't expect to be welcomed with open arms just because you were successful in the for-profit world. Seek out nonprofits looking for people with business experience, which can help the nonprofit achieve its goals.

- Know what you can do for the field you are getting into by having a complete understanding of the organization's goals and expectations.

- Be realistic about your salary, vacation, and benefits. Look at resources such as Salary.com to give you a sense of the salaries in the field you are looking at. Salaries tend to be 20 to 50 percent lower than in the for-profit world. Visit the Association of Fundraising Professionals site (afpnet.org) to learn more about compensation and other issues.

• Get training. Credentials help in the nonprofit world, and there's a lot to learn. It's important to keep in mind that a nonprofit degree or certificate can add $20,000 to $40,000 to earnings. A number of people complete a master's in social work in their fifties. There are roughly thirty programs that grant master's degrees in nonprofit study. (Many programs offer night courses, so with some effort, you can fit them into your existing work and personal life.) More than another hundred programs offer degrees in public administration, philanthropic studies, and social work—some can even be earned completely online. A listing of undergraduate, graduate, and certificate programs is provided by Seton Hall University (academic.shu.edu/npo/list.php). Some institutions that offer training include New York University, Columbia University, Case Western Reserve University, Indiana University, Seton Hall University, and the University of San Francisco. Course work includes nonprofit marketing, fundraising, campaigns, corporate philanthropy, ethics, and law.

• Know yourself. You need a certain amount of humility. Decisions are usually made by consensus, so if you are an independent operator, this might not be a good fit. You can't allow yourself to get discouraged easily. In the nonprofit world, you work hard, and there are usually never enough resources to make it all happen as quickly or successfully as you would want. And if you're a go-getter-make-things-happen-fast kind of worker, *whoa*—a nonprofit can test your patience to the *n*th degree.

- Check out websites such as Commongood Careers (cgcareers .org) and the Bridgespan Group (bridgespan.org). Such organizations help executives make the transition to nonprofits and are excellent sources for people with general skill sets to shift into the nonprofit world. They list board opportunities and contacts for headhunters looking for individuals who can play executive roles in nonprofits.

EXPERT ADVICE

Betsy Werley, The Transition Network

After twenty-five years of plying her legal expertise, first at law firms and later at JPMorgan Chase, Betsy Werley was ready for a change. She took a deep breath and made the leap from corporate lawyer to a position as the executive director of the Transition Network, a New York City–based nonprofit whose aim is helping women over fifty make career changes. She was one month shy of her fiftieth birthday. "I thought, gee, I'm turning fifty," Werley said. "I'm not getting any younger. Go out and let that next big thing happen." In reality, it didn't happen that fast. It evolved gradually over a period of five or six years as she focused on how to try something new. "I always thought about a job in the nonprofit world," she said. "Even when I was at JPMorgan Chase, I was involved in networking projects for women."

First, she began by looking for boards to get involved with as a volunteer. She joined the Financial Women's Association and in 2001 was named its president. "I wasn't necessarily planning a career in nonprofit work at the time, but I knew it would open up a lot of opportunities," she says.

Having had a taste of leadership experience, she became convinced that she *did* want to work for a nonprofit and, more important, for a much smaller organization.

So while Werley kept up her duties at JPMorgan Chase, she got busy prepping for her next act. She enrolled in courses at New York University. She drafted up a new résumé. And she did the footwork. "I talked to a lot of people in the nonprofit world to understand where I might be a fit and see if my credentials made sense," she says. "Some of that was basic social networking," she says. Whether it was a party or professional function, Werley got out there and let people know what she was interested in.

And she hit the Internet. She surfed onto BoardnetUSA (board netusa.org), a website for anyone looking for a nonprofit board. It's a single collection point for organizations that are seeking new board members. "It has a terrific search engine," Werley says. "Individuals can post where they are located, what kind of mission and organization they are looking for, and what their skill set is. Once you've posted your information, you get a weekly email with a list of organizations looking for people who fit your profile."

At the same time, through the Financial Women's Association, she linked up with a couple of women who were doing consulting for nonprofit boards. "I told them about my interests, which were initially in two areas—using technology to enable people to solve problems and women," she recalls.

She used her network to meet with people and say, "Here's the kind of organization I am looking for. Who do you know of and what's their reputation, and could you make an introduction?" Once she was in the door, Werley was able to talk with people who were doing the work she was interested in.

It was enlightening. "I learned about different kinds of jobs, different sizes of organizations, and had people in those jobs tell me about how they got there and talk to me about myself as a candidate for those organizations," Werley says. Bit by bit she narrowed down her choices.

Among the people she talked with were Charlotte Frank and Christine Millen, cofounders of the Transition Network, a group for women in circumstances much like her own. The tipping point came when her longtime employer offered her a package of a year's salary plus a year's benefits. It was her chance to make the break, and it coincided with an offer from TTN.

At the heart of it for Werley is the quest for meaning—which she believes comes in many different forms. "It can certainly be the mission of an organization," she says, "but I think meaning can also come from working for a smaller organization, where you make much more of a contribution. You don't feel you are a cog in a huge machine. And you have more control over what you are doing."

At the Transition Network, she was the second employee.

||||||||||

NETWORKING

One of the hidden opportunities of looking for second acts is the ability to tap into the network you have been creating over the years. Your experience means you have more resources to draw on than people in their twenties and thirties. Here's how to work it:

- *Send out a blast email* using a tool like "mail merge" in Microsoft Word to personalize each message. Let your friends and associates know that you are thinking of changing careers, quickly list some of your work background and expertise to date, and let them in on the direction you are heading. But, of course, be discreet if you're currently employed. You wouldn't want to have someone on that list who might spill the beans to your boss.

- *Mine alumni associations* to track down fellow grads—even if you haven't spoken to classmates in years, people tend to want to assist those who share a common background. Be sure to check out the fine print in the class notes section of alumni magazines to see if someone has recently been promoted or has sent in an update on their current work and personal lives.

- *Update your online profiles* on LinkedIn, Facebook, Google+, and Twitter to signal your new career track. Online networking and rah-rah self-promotion through social media channels is a little awkward for many of us, but with practice it gets easier. "Social media is one of the easiest ways to accomplish several key factors that help people land jobs," Miriam Salpeter, a job search and social media coach, owner of Keppie Careers and author of *Social Networking for Career Success: Using Online Tools to Create a Personal Brand*, says. "There's no easier way to showcase what you know to a broad audience of potential colleagues, networking contacts, and hiring managers than via using social media." Get connected with a LinkedIn group dedicated to your next career, to learn about trends and timely topics. Join in. If you've read a terrific article— share it with your connections as an update. It illustrates that you're continually learning new things. "Statistically speaking, we know that if you share once a week you increase your chances of having your profile viewed by a recruiter tenfold," says LinkedIn's career expert Nicole Williams.

- *Review LinkedIn profiles* of other professionals in your field and see how they've described their work. You will find keywords to include in your summary description, or ways to describe the work you do in a smart, non-jargon way.

- When it comes to social media, make sure you abide by the following:

  » Pick the right headshot, a current one that makes you look engaged, vibrant, and professional.

  » Tread lightly. Be careful. It's all about good taste and decorum. Even when you're posting pictures from your vacation or of your lovely Labrador retriever (as I'm known to do) or commenting on a high school pal's post, pause before you push the post button. What you do online is not like Vegas. It doesn't just stay there. It floats out into the virtual airspace, and it's, well, virtually impossible to reel it in. Your online personality reflects who you are. It's all part of your personal brand like wearing a seersucker suit in the summer. It's OK to list your hobbies and comment or post articles you find interesting, but keep it in good taste.

  » Don't adopt a laissez-faire attitude toward your online social media footprint on sites such as LinkedIn, Facebook, and Twitter. A recent CareerBuilder nationwide survey found that more than two in five hiring managers who use social media to research potential employees said they found information online that caused them not to hire a candidate. The biggest turnoffs for potential employers: Candidate posted provocative or inappropriate photos or information—50 percent. Sites had information about candidate drinking or using drugs—48 percent. Candidate bad-mouthed previous employer—33 percent. Candidate had poor communication skills—30 percent. Candidate made discriminatory comments related to race, gender, or religion—28 percent. Candidate lied about qualifications—24 percent. In today's job market, you must have an online profile, though. And it can work for you, if you manage your accounts diligently. Accept that social media is one piece of your job hunt and don't let your guard down. Never forget that everything that you post online tells your story. Make it a bestseller.

» Build your network with people who know you from high school, college, and throughout your working life. Trust me, they can turn out to be great sources when you're job hunting. You never know where you might get an introduction to a potential employer, or hear of a job opening.

» Do a web search through the networking sites to see if you know anyone who's already working in the field you're interested in.

» Show your expertise. There's no easier way to showcase what you know to a broad audience of potential colleagues, networking contacts, and hiring managers than via social media. For example, post a link to a relevant article on your LinkedIn or Facebook page with your own short commentary or tweet it to your Twitter followers. Chime in on a LinkedIn group discussion, even if it means merely checking the "Like" button. Social media makes it easier for people to learn about you, and that's necessary to land a job.

- Whether online or in person, you *can* ask others for help without being pushy. It's as simple as asking for an introduction to someone who works in your future arena—offer to treat the person to coffee or a drink in exchange for some helpful information or informally exchange emails if an in-person meeting is not in the cards. You might also ask for any leads on professional groups or job opportunities. Keep your requests short and sweet, and be grateful to anyone who responds.

CHAPTER EIGHT

Barking Up the Right Tree

As a kid, Deborah Langsam used to stare in the windows of the bakeries in Brooklyn, New York, and dream of what delicacies she would buy if she had all the money in the world.

As co-owner of Barking Dog Chocolatiers, an artisanal chocolate company in Charlotte, North Carolina, Langsam, a former associate professor of biology, no longer has to fantasize about indulging her sweet tooth. With her husband, Joal Fischer, a retired developmental pediatrician, she stirs up vats of silky chocolate and handcrafts it into mouth-watering truffles, barks, ganaches, and pastries in a state-of-the-art home kitchen.

Langsam, a botanist, retired after twenty-two years at the University of North Carolina at Charlotte. Fischer officially shuttered his medical practice fifteen years ago to focus on SupportWorks, a nonprofit clearinghouse he founded to help people find and form support groups and research medical information.

Before retiring from science and medicine, the couple took a six-week pastry course at the École Ritz Escoffier in Paris, alongside professional chefs. It was in the basement of the tony Ritz hotel that they fell madly in love with the process of making chocolate. It's no surprise that it was the science that intrigued them—the methodical experiments and technical precision needed to ensure a ganache that was smooth, not grainy.

Eventually, they journeyed around the United States, Canada, and beyond to train with expert pastry chefs and chocolatiers, honing the techniques of framing, molding, and panning. Finally, they began designing their own chocolates.

Their tempting morsels were a resounding success with friends, who pushed the couple to make chocolates to sell. Soon they officially started Barking Dog Chocolatiers, naming it in honor of a favorite pooch that barked only when she was hungry.

Annual candy sales fluctuate each year, but the sweet news is that all profits (neither Langsam nor Fischer earns a salary from Barking Dog) go to local charities. These charities include SupportWorks; Friendship Trays (friendshiptrays.org), a group that delivers more than six hundred meals daily to elderly, handicapped, and convalescing people who are unable or greatly restricted in their ability to prepare or secure meals; and NC MedAssist (medassist.org), a nonprofit that assists low-income, uninsured North Carolina residents by operating a licensed pharmacy that provides free medication, healthcare advocacy, and related educational services. Everyone is a volunteer—no salaries are paid.

It's a small business, and the couple aim to keep it that way. The chocolate making is still a two-person operation. In spurts, they might spend fifteen hours a day swirling up their elegant chocolates to fill customer orders from their website—sampler boxes, wedding novelties, or special orders with custom logos. And their candies and pastries are served as dessert at the Bonterra Dining & Wine Room, a Charlotte restaurant.

Their latest confection: the St. Bernard Collection, decadent milk and dark chocolate truffles. The new candies sell for $22 for a box of ten truffles, but they can also be purchased at a $5 discount, "a mitzvah price" for those ordering for anyone with a very serious illness.

"For someone who is going through chemotherapy, for instance, or someone who is having trouble chewing, the truffles are easy to eat because they melt in your mouth," Langsam explains. "We created them for a dear friend who was battling cancer. The feedback has been amazing. And that's exactly why we do what we do."

There's plenty of downtime for Langsam to spend on her fabric art business, called Barking Dog Fiber Arts, which has taken off with juried and solo art gallery shows. All profits from those sales also go to charity. Plus there's allotted time for Fischer to tend to SupportWorks, as well as for the duo to travel and take more chocolate courses. "We don't measure our self-worth by how much money comes in," Fischer says. "We don't want to get caught up in the American way of always getting bigger and bigger."

Langsam's decision to retire from academia stemmed in large part from "the constant pressure to do more," she says. "There was always another paper to write, a bigger grant to be awarded."

Deciding to leave her faculty post, even with full retirement benefits, wasn't easy. "I liked what I did very much," she says. "My identity was as a professor." Yet an early health scare with cancer, when she was in her thirties, had taught Langsam how short life can be.

Was it really worth working so hard to be named a full professor? "It was an ego thing for me," Langsam says.

Sensible spending suits the couple's sweet new lifestyle—and they had always made do on modest salaries. They both drive teenage Volvos and don't splurge on designer clothes or fancy jewelry.

"There is no way we could have planned this adventure," Fischer says. "It started out as a kick, something fun to do together. Now all we have to say is that we make chocolate and everyone smiles!"

I asked Debbie and Joal to look back and share their thoughts on their transition to chocolatiers.

What did the transition mean to you personally?

Debbie: At first it scared me because it meant I was giving up my identity as a professor. But the career change has allowed me to enjoy my work and the process of creating something. Every once in a while I'll be on a deadline, and it reminds me of how much my life was once controlled by deadlines. It reminds me of how much I get pleasure from what I am doing now.

Joal: Now we have second acts in which we are able to work hard when we want—and then take a break. A couple years ago, we worked eighteen hours a day, six or seven days a week, getting the candy out. It keeps us really busy, but for relatively short periods of time, and then we're done. We love it.

Were you confident that you were doing the right thing? Any second-guessing?

Debbie: Once I left the university, there was no second-guessing. I have never regretted it for a minute. I've missed certain things. One of the things I really loved about my university work was teaching. But now Joal and I do chocolate tasting and teach chocolate-making techniques in small groups, so I get to do some of that in other ways.

Anything you would have done differently?

Joal: No. Well, there's always . . . wouldn't it have been nice to have started this a year earlier?

How do you measure your success?

Joal: We don't take it for granted.

How big a role did financial rewards play in your decision to make a transition?

Debbie: None—in the sense that we didn't need to make money to live on, so it wasn't as stressful. Even though we took a financial hit in our retirement accounts, we still feel we have enough saved to meet our needs. We live responsibly. We are able to say no to things that don't work for us and say yes to things that would be a good adventure. As a child of Depression-era parents, I had to get over my fear that we didn't have enough saved before I left the university job. But we're doing fine. It's all about giving back.

Joal: Money is important in many ways, but it's not always the answer. For example, Costco contacted us about selling our chocolate, but we felt it would create too much stress and work. So we said no.

How did your preparation help you succeed?

Joal: I stepped out of my practice in stages and was able to gradually learn about cooking and making chocolate. We traveled and studied chocolate making by taking classes from masters. That was a no-brainer. Why not learn from people who have been doing this for thirty or forty years? It was obvious that we needed to do some kind of training, and the training was fun. Through various connections, I was able to volunteer at Dean & Deluca, making chocolate. I happened to be there on the day they needed an extra hand, and I just stayed on.

We overplanned things financially so we could afford to make the change. The planning allowed this to be an adventure that could take on a life of its own. We're able to make chocolate for people who are sick—that's fantastic. Whatever good works come out of this is wonderful.

Debbie: I want to add that we started small. At the very beginning we made chocolate for friends and relatives. Then we sold it at the restaurant here in Charlotte. Then we thought about starting a website. But we didn't jump in, start a website, and then try to get publicity. We had the luxury of being satisfied with small triumphs along the way. It has all evolved in its own time.

What do you tell people who ask for your advice?

Joal: You want to make chocolate? Great! Do you like to wash dishes? Hmm. You have to really understand the details. In our case, it means painstakingly measuring out ingredients and cleaning up. Any business has day-to-day details that are repetitive in nature. So pick a profession where you can tolerate the grunt work the best. I really do like to measure! And I don't have a problem with dish detail.

What books or resources did you use or recommend others to use?

> "The planning allowed this to be an adventure that could take on a life of its own. We're able to make chocolate for people who are sick—that's fantastic. Whatever good works come out of this is wonderful."

Debbie: The Internet. Online chat groups and shopping online vendors for all the resources we need to fuel our passion.

Joal: Our biggest resource was and is each other.

What are some of the surprises and unexpected rewards?

Debbie: There have been so many. I had no idea that things were going to open up for me as an artist. I had no idea that I would be doing shows or that one of my pieces would be used as a publicity shot for a gallery show. The biggest joy has been seeing doors open that we hadn't planned, seeing doors appear that we never thought about. Like having an article about us in *U.S. News & World Report*!

Joal: This whole adventure has been a surprise.

Educational Vacations

If you're interested in a new craft or trade, take a trip that lets you come home with more than a bunch of photos. Educational vacations such as the cooking vacations that Debbie Langsam and Joal Fischer took before embarking in their chocolate business are a great way to study with the masters and, well, get a taste of a potential new line of work.

Typically a week or two long, these intense training sessions with professionals allow you to accumulate experience while you are still working at your current job. They can be a great way to build the expertise and proficiency needed for a new career. They can be pricey, but far less than you might spend if you enrolled in a full-time degree program at a local college.

The sheer variety of offerings worldwide is mind numbing. Serious cooks might want to thumb through the *Guide to Culinary Arts Programs & Career Cooking Schools* published by ShawGuides (shaw guides.com). It contains detailed descriptions of more than a thousand schools, colleges, culinary apprenticeships, cooking vacations, and wine programs worldwide. The comprehensive ShawGuide has more. It's divided into two sections: one for career programs and one for recreational programs.

Want to become a bagpiper? There are two-week courses taught by world-class piper instructors at the North American Academy of Piping and Drumming in Valle Crucis, North Carolina. Whet your woodcarving, quilting, or doll-making skills at Fletcher Farm School for the Arts and Crafts in Ludlow, Vermont, which offers five-day courses. You can also sign up for an arduous two-week course in carpentry, furniture building, landscaping, or stone masonry and learn to *really* build homes at Yestermorrow Design/Build School in Warren, Vermont.

To find out more about various learning vacations, check out the ShawGuides website for a smorgasbord of courses. Established in 1988 as a publisher of comprehensive worldwide guides to educational travel and creative career programs, ShawGuides offers free online access to the unabridged, continually updated content.

EXPERT ADVICE

Emily Dewhirst, The Age-Friendly Peace Corps

Emily Dewhirst, the oldest Peace Corps volunteer in service, is in her eighties. Dewhirst, of Knoxville, Tennessee, is currently serving her third assignment with the organization as a Peace Corps Response volunteer in Moldova.

To me, the Peace Corps (peacecorps.gov) has always stood out as a very groovy thing to have on your résumé. But it seemed like a young person's game—something to do right out of college. That's simply not the case these days, midcareer folks and retirees like Dewhirst are increasingly taking up the quest. I decided to contact her to find out why she does it. Before I did, though, I had to show my geographic ignorance. Where exactly is Moldova?

Moldova, officially the Republic of Moldova, is a landlocked nation in eastern Europe located between Romania to the west and Ukraine to the north, east, and south.

It sounds pretty exotic to me, so I asked a public affairs specialist at the Peace Corps for details. Apparently, just over a thousand Peace Corps volunteers have served in Moldova since 1993, and right now, there about 120 volunteers there working in the areas of English education, health, business development, and community development. The volunteers, like Dewhirst, are trained to speak and work in Romanian and Russian.

I emailed Dewhirst to ask her about her experience.

What motivates you to keep volunteering?

Dewhirst: For the answer, you had to be with me Friday when I taught at the orphanage in a small town in Moldova. There were fifteen adorable children, starved for love and attention, who endure a brutal world of often uncaring people. The fifth graders were full of fun and joy that Friday and wishing my university girls and I would stay forever. My heart was in my throat all the time we taught there. Their need is so apparent, so urgent. So I am here.

Is there an advantage to your age?

Dewhirst: The advantage of being older certainly includes the fact that age is revered in the countries where I have worked. People look at me and appreciate the expertise and experience I bring. They are more inclined to believe I can share meaningful ways of doing things.

When did you get involved with the Peace Corps?

Dewhirst: I took my first Peace Corps assignment in Kazakhstan at the age of sixty-three, when I served for two years teaching English and working with English teachers to improve their skills. At age eighty-one, I served in Armenia for seven months as part of Peace Corps Response, where I developed and taught a series of

English classes that were used in my village's schools and replicated throughout Armenia at other Peace Corps posts. In October of this year, I headed to Moldova for my second Peace Corps Response assignment, where I will focus on improving English education for teachers and students.

What is Peace Corps Response?

Dewhirst: It's a program that provides opportunities for qualified Americans to undertake short-term, high-impact assignments in various sectors around the world. Peace Corps Response (peacecorps.gov/response) assignments last between three months and one year with an opportunity to extend based on program needs.

It's uniquely suited to me. I can commit for a shorter time, and I am able to use my talents where they are needed and wanted.

Do you recommend this kind of work to your peers?

Dewhirst: No matter what your age, I encourage anyone who wants to commit to making a difference in the lives of others to apply for the Peace Corps. If you're really interested in other people, learning from them, then this is the job for you. What we bring to the lives of others is our creativity, our openness, and our energy.

||||||||||

THE NITTY-GRITTY ABOUT THE PEACE CORPS

Currently, more than 7 percent of Peace Corps volunteers are over the age of fifty and are serving in sixty-one posts worldwide. Since President John F. Kennedy established the Peace Corps by executive order on March 1, 1961, more than 210,000 Americans have served in 139 host countries.

Today, more than eight thousand volunteers are working with local communities in 76 countries in agriculture, community economic development, education, environment, health, and youth in development. Peace Corps volunteers must be U.S. citizens and at least eighteen years old.

While Peace Corps Volunteers do not get paid a salary, Peace Corps provides volunteers with an allowance to cover housing, food, and incidentals. It also provides complete dental and medical care during service, including shots, vaccinations, and medicines. And, of course, it covers the cost of transportation to and from the country of service.

While I am doubtful that I will ever head to exotic lands like Moldova to work, I can't help but wonder what kind of job I will I be doing at age eighty. How about you?

CHAPTER NINE

A Road Map for Women in Retirement

Charlotte Frank remembers heading downtown on a brilliant September morning toward her office in lower Manhattan, where she was an executive with the Port Authority of New York and New Jersey.

She never made it. Her office was in the North Tower of the World Trade Center, and it was September 11, 2001. She couldn't get past Canal Street. She stood with dozens of onlookers and watched the first tower collapse. They uttered almost in unison, "Oh . . . my . . . God."

Frank retired the next year at sixty-seven, after helping the agency get back on its feet. "I was on my way out," she says. "But that precipitated it. You never know what's going to happen, so you better get on with what you really want to do, your next act."

She got on with it. Within days, she was working full time with no pay for the Transition Network, a New York nonprofit for women over fifty who are at or near retirement. Frank had founded the group two years earlier with her friend Christine Millen, then fifty-eight and a partner at the consulting firm Deloitte & Touche.

Frank and Millen had spent many lunches trying to sort out what to do with their own retirements. They came to realize that they were on the leading edge of a generation of women better educated and more ambitious than any before. These were the first women to have reached top-level positions in business, government, and other fields, and they were facing possibly thirty years of retirement—without a road map. "We asked ourselves, What do you do when you don't have a purpose? What do you do when you don't have your career? What do you do when you don't have your identity? Your social network? It's a time of major loss."

Frank and Millen launched the fledgling outfit with no budget, staff, or office space—but with a firm belief that they were onto something big. The women broadly define retirement as a series of transitions—a bridge from one career to another or from employment to volunteerism, advocacy, or community—a grassroots movement that "reimagines retirement." The challenge was to build networking groups to provide support and share information. "I wanted to continue to have an impact on the world and needed an organizational structure to do so," Frank says. "I always felt I could change the world taking on large issues and large groups of people."

Frank still thinks big. Today, the Transition Network has more than eight thousand members in eleven states, with chapters in Atlanta, Boston, Chicago, San Francisco, and Santa Fe. New chapters are forming in Phoenix, Fort Lauderdale, Portland, and Dayton, Ohio. (For details, send an email to info@thetransitionnetwork

.org.) Memberships costs $70 to $135 a year if there is a chapter in your city, $40 if not.

Frank came of age as a feminist in an era when a woman was encouraged to get an education and use it—to further her *husband's* career. "My mother actually told me not to show my intelligence if I wanted to get a man," she says, laughing. That is one piece of advice Charlotte Frank wisely ignored.

_____

I asked Charlotte to look back and share her thoughts on her transition to founding and running a nonprofit.

What did the transition mean to you personally?

I am driven by a compulsion to do something, usually something that helps society cope with its problems. I'm not driven by accumulating wealth—I never was. When I worked for the government, I probably made $100,000 less than I would have in the private sector. I am blessed with a really good pension, so I could pursue what really mattered to me.

Were you confident that you were doing the right thing? Any second-guessing?

I didn't know anything about running an organization or business planning, but I always thought our direction was right. I knew we were onto something big.

I admit it was a struggle for the first five years to bring in money. Finally, it was too much. That's when we committed to an executive director and started running it like a business. It was a great learning experience, and we've never looked back.

Anything you would have done differently?

Not really. I wish we could have afforded to hire a director sooner. It was only when things started exploding in terms of growth that we realized we needed to step back and start thinking about raising money. Is it through contributions? Grants? Dues?

How did your preparation help you succeed?

I have always been in a state of learning and just kept on going after I retired. You must be in a constant state of learning to succeed.

What do you tell people who ask for your advice?

You need to be engaged with people. Try to connect with a network of peers or a community. Don't try to figure out what's next alone. You really have to open up, even though you might feel vulnerable. You have to connect, and you have to develop relationships.

Look for interesting volunteer opportunities. Regardless of whether you retire late, take an early-retirement package, or are laid off, you have a chance to really change your life. Volunteering can really shape your second act. It might lead directly to a specific job, or it might lead to a vision of a job. In my case, it led to the founding of an organization.

TTN was my second act. The Caring Collaborative is my third act. I have no idea what my fourth act is going to be, but I have every intention of having one. In my fourth act, though, I am going to do things that are totally irresponsible because I have been totally responsible my entire life.

What books or resources did you use or recommend others to use?

Smart Women Don't Retire— They Break Free: From Working Full-Time to Living Full-Time and *An Optimist's Guide to Retirement.*

> "We asked ourselves, 'What do you do when you don't have a purpose? What do you do when you don't have your career? What do you do when you don't have your identity? . . . It's a time of major loss."

What are some of the surprises and unexpected rewards?

It is without a doubt the formation of the Caring Collaborative, a TTN New York City pilot project.

In 2006, I was diagnosed with cancer and had surgery to remove my thyroid gland. I suddenly lost my voice and couldn't catch my breath—my vocal cords had become paralyzed as a side effect of the surgery. I had no energy and no appetite. I was seventy-three years old, living in an apartment in midtown Manhattan, where I have been for more than twenty years, and had no family nearby. My friends helped me by bringing home-cooked meals, grocery shopping, and coming along to my doctors' appointments to take notes, be my advocate, and even help pick up prescriptions at the pharmacy. I would never have asked them to do all that, but they knew I needed help.

I realized then that you have to learn how to use your network when you need it. Some people don't learn how to ask for help until it's almost too late. As we get older, we need each other even more.

The Caring Collaborative is like a time bank—jump-started with help from the Visiting Nurse Service of New York, a home-health nonprofit. Each member earns an hour of credit by volunteering to help another member in need. Those credits can be redeemed for help with health problems later. Since the inception hundreds of volunteers have signed up.

VOLUNTEER TOWARD YOUR SECOND ACT

Before you sign on to volunteer with an organization, here are some questions to consider:

- What kind of organization or company fits with the career field you are hoping to explore? Interested in getting into the music business? Volunteering as a docent at a performing arts center can get you backstage and face to face with performers and their entourages. Want to start your own winery? Volunteer to work at a local vineyard during harvest time or help pour in the tasting room. Love to cook? How about offering to be a sous-chef at a nearby restaurant, free of charge?

- What size organization would suit you? Do you prefer a small group with a narrow focus and fewer resources but greater opportunity to make a difference? Or are you drawn to a larger organization, which might offer skilled training and more potential job openings but less hands-on work?

- How deep do you want to dig in? Do you want to be out in the field working directly with people or would you rather develop strategies in an office? How much time can you commit? Weekends? Full-time?

- How long of a commitment do you want to make? If you're just getting started, it's wise to seek a project with a clear time frame of six months or less.

- Are you prepared to approach this as you would a paying job? That means pulling together a résumé, interviewing, and dedicating yourself to all the professional skills and expertise you have nurtured and developed throughout your career.

THINKING OF STARTING A NONPROFIT ORGANIZATION?

Starting a nonprofit can be an especially complicated process, but the payoff can be deeply rewarding. One of the leading resources to help you get going is Idealist (idealist.org). This website offers in-depth guidance, lays out first steps for launching a new organization, and provides resources. According to Idealist, generally speaking, you will know you have a solid case for starting a new nonprofit if:

- You have a clientele or beneficiary with a bona fide need that's not being met by an existing nonprofit or program.

- You have an innovative programming idea or approach to meeting the need.

- You already have (or know how you can secure) the monetary and in-kind donations needed to support the organization for the foreseeable future.

You know you have the right amount of passion, but do you have what it takes? The answer may be yes, if:

- You have thoroughly researched the industry and field you are entering and have a solid plan of action.

- You have spent plenty of ample boots-on-the-ground time understanding the world of nonprofits, being out in the community working with other nonprofits, and interacting with other people who started nonprofits to glean their perspective and experience.

- You have completed the IRS paperwork for establishing a nonprofit entity. IRS publication 557 contains information on all the organizational categories and instructions on qualifying for and applying for 501(c) status.

- Funding to launch your company and sustain it for an adequate period is in place.

THE PERSONAL TOLL OF NONPROFITS

Even if you have a grasp of the nuts and bolts of launching a nonprofit, be sure to consider the personal downside of delving into this kind of work before you commit. Here are some of the stark realities, as pointed out in *The Idealist Guide to Nonprofit Careers for Sector Switchers*:

- Burnout is not to be taken lightly. Starting this kind of venture typically demands long hours, low or no pay, and the final responsibility for your project's success falls to you and you alone. And don't hold your breath for all the back-slapping for a job well done. It may be years before your organization's work is acknowledged, if it ever is.

- As the founder of a nonprofit, you are typically the face of the organization. That means you need to be prepared for public exposure.

- You will need to be at ease asking friends, relatives, community members, and those in your network for support. You will need absolutely everyone you know to be by your side to spread the word and shore you up to push through some of those long days.

- Be aware of your time commitment. As the founder, you might play a huge and active role in the early days, but eventually you will need to have a plan in place to step off the stage. Making room for a new generation of leaders to take the reins is never easy, but it's critical to sustaining an organization over time. Then too be careful not to lose your own identity in that of the nonprofit. With all of the time, energy, and passion that go into starting and nourishing a nonprofit, drawing the line between yourself and the organization can be harder than you think. This kind of work is personal and takes passion. Learn to make the space between.

Fundraising

If you have a great idea and have done all the legwork to start your nonprofit, this is where the rubber meets the road. How do you pay for it all? Fundraising is a key ingredient to your ultimate success and requires nurturing a rapport with donors, establishing a database of existing and potential donors, and attracting, training, and motivating volunteers. Other key aspects include writing grant proposals, overseeing email and phone campaigns, and running fundraising events from galas to film screenings.

Here are two websites to help you learn the ropes and connect you with potential donors:

The Association of Fundraising Professionals (afpnet.org) represents over thirty thousand members in 235 chapters throughout the United States, Canada, Mexico, and China, working to advance philanthropy through training courses, advocacy, research, education, and certification programs.

The Foundation Center (foundationcenter.org) educates thousands of people each year through a full curriculum of training courses—in the classroom and online. Free and affordable classes nationwide cover grant proposal writing and fundraising skills. The center also maintains databases of information on the foundations, corporate donors, and grant-making public charities in the United States and their recent grants.

The site consists of a variety of free search tools, tutorials, downloadable reports, and other information updated daily, including the Philanthropy News Digest, its daily news service. The foundation also offers webinars ranging from basic primers on fundraising to winning grants.

Take a Course in Fundraising

One way to sharpen your fundraising skills is to enroll in classes offered by the Foundation Center and the Association of Fundraising Professionals (AFP). Many colleges and universities also offer courses in fundraising.

The AFP's (afpnet.org) Essentials of Fundraising series offers introductory-level sessions—five three-hour interactive workshops—to introduce the novice fundraiser to the fundamental concepts and techniques of fundraising. Volunteers, too, will find the Essentials of Fundraising helpful in learning how to approach potential donors for contributions.

Here are some areas the workshops cover:

- Starting a development program
- Identifying and soliciting annual donors
- Seeking grant support
- Developing a board and volunteer base
- Securing individual major gifts

The workshops allow you to develop skills that can be customized to fit your organization. Moreover, you'll have the opportunity to network and develop relationships with other fundraisers in your area. And there are plenty of takeaway tools such as sample fundraising plans, solicitation letters, policies, and guidelines to jump-start your efforts.

CHAPTER TEN

Build It and They Will Come

Jay Goldberg's passion for his work was fueled early on. Goldberg was three years old when his dad, an avid baseball fan, took him to his first baseball game. The year was 1963, and Whitey Ford was pitching.

Queens-native Goldberg, now fifty-three, spent most of that day crawling under seats looking for bottle caps with pictures of professional ballplayers glued onto the cork linings.

He admits, though, that his first real memory of the game is from the following year, when he clutched a Mr. Met doll and clung to his dad's hand as they walked down the huge Shea Stadium concrete concourse.

A prescient moment. Today, Goldberg is the owner of New York City's Bergino Baseball Clubhouse in Greenwich Village.

After graduating from New York University, he kicked off his career as a political consultant working with legendary political guru David Garth for six years.

It was a tremendous experience, but it was the sports world that called to Goldberg. With a little legwork, he managed to redeploy his political strategy skills to a position as a professional sports agent. That gig lasted for about fifteen years (first with a big firm, and then several years on his own).

But to be an agent you have to be driven by money, not passion, says Goldberg. "It actually took away my great passion of being a sports fan."

He knew in his heart he couldn't be robbed of his love for baseball. He swung for the fences.

In 2001, Goldberg started a business manufacturing and wholesaling a line of baseball-related gift items. Admittedly, he was an ingenue. He didn't, for example, realize at first that his typical customer was ultimately a woman buying a novelty gift for a man, not a man buying for himself.

"I didn't know anything about manufacturing," he recalls. "I didn't know how to make a baseball. I didn't know I was getting into the gift business. I just thought a customized painted baseball was cool."

What he did know was that he didn't enjoy what he was doing as an agent. "I had this idea, and I started," he remembers matter-of-factly. "The first baseballs we made looked terrible," he admits with a laugh. "They were like squashed oranges."

But he was tenacious. In time, Goldberg started making other items such as drink coasters made from AstroTurf, and tiny baseball glove business-card holders. And in time, his products were widely sold in boutiques, department stores, and museum shops around the country.

One downside: It was solitary work. His main interaction with people and customers was at the big trade shows—which came around only a handful of times each year.

In 2010, Goldberg decided he needed a change. He didn't necessarily want to abandon the business, but he had a serious itch to do something else. He toyed with becoming a designer—took a few classes at Parsons to feel that out—but that wasn't right.

Ultimately, he decided to take his existing business in a new direction and opened a retail store, event space, and art gallery all focused on baseball. He admits that he was inspired by the intimate tiny shops he and his wife had visited while honeymooning in Lisbon. Goldberg sought available spaces in Manhattan and found a vacancy in the Cast Iron Building. "My vision was to have an art gallery as an homage to baseball." One of the upsides of the recession was that retail rents were low, so he got a good deal on space.

Why retail? "I would go into a store to see how the products I was making, for example, the baseballs, were displayed and get upset," Goldberg recalls. "I thought, I can do this better."

Arrogance, maybe, but it was that drive that sent him to the next base. For Goldberg, by far the best part of this new career is that he runs a literary series with baseball writers and hosts regular art shows featuring baseball artists.

In just two years, the Clubhouse has become a gathering place for people who love the game, especially those who are interested in the history and those involved in baseball in various ways. These loyal patrons run the gamut from collectors of memorabilia to ex-professional ball players to today's Little Leaguers, who still sleep with a leather glove under their pillow.

However, he has all the stresses of a running a retail business. There are, for instance, those mornings when the garbage doesn't get picked up, and he has to push it aside to open the front door. Nonetheless, he gets a huge kick out of going to work every day—which he does six days a week. He has no employees, by choice, so when he's off, the 750-square-foot Clubhouse is closed.

"I've always had a passion for work. I have never been motivated by a paycheck, and I have always loved what I have done," Goldberg says. What energizes him today is that the store has become a community gathering spot for people who love baseball from all walks of life. "We celebrate baseball," he proclaims. "The door will spring open and nearly everybody will have a smile on their face, and they will have a smile on their face the entire time they're in here," he says. "That's really a great thing. I take a lot of pride in that."

And sweetly enough, Bergino Baseball Clubhouse has become a gathering place for a range of baseball fans from the members of the New York Baseball Giants Nostalgia Society to newcomers to the game to fathers and sons who appreciate the art and handmade collectibles. Like him, Goldberg says that nearly everyone he speaks to in his shop recalls how he first learned a love of the game from his pop.

And it's that human interaction that keeps him opening the store each morning. "Meeting new people keeps the job interesting," he says. "And the learning curve never really stops. You keep making a lot of mistakes."

Indeed, it does, plus he has a ten-year lease. "That should take me through my fifties. You never know. It wouldn't shock me if I go full circle and my work leads me back to politics where I still feel a passion."

Goldberg's advice for others: "As soon as you start asking yourself, is this all there is to my job, it's already time to go. If you have a tolerance for risk, you will go for it. You need more than passion, though, you have to be willing to do hard work on top of the passion."

In fact, Goldberg admits if he weren't married, he'd probably be there seven days a week.

Final score: One day a customer walked into the Clubhouse, looked around at what he saw, and blurted out: "There can't be any other store like this in the whole world."

"That's what makes it all worthwhile," Goldberg says proudly.

Play ball.

I asked Jay to look back and share his thoughts on his transition to a career as small business retailer.

What did the transition mean to you personally?

It felt like it was a challenge that I wanted to be up for—to give it a shot. It was the right time, and I was excited about that next step. I enjoy the work, even though there are a lot more challenges owning a retail shop and gallery.

Were you confident that you were doing the right thing? Any second-guessing?

I never second-guessed myself. For everything I've done I've always felt it was the right time and time to move on from what I was doing before.

Anything you would have done differently?

There's a lot I would have done differently but that doesn't mean I would second-guess it. I have learned from experience, so of course, many things I would do differently. But I don't look back and say "I wish I had done it that way." I did it the best I could at that time. I hope I keep learning. What's the point otherwise?

How do you measure your success?

It is not financial. It never was for me in anything I've done. It has really been about enjoying it. I know it is a success if I never think of doing something else. Once I am, then I know I am not really into it 100 percent anymore. That is how I judge—that I thoroughly enjoy it.

How big a role did financial rewards play in your decision to make a transition?

That did not play into it at all. It has never factored into it.

How did your preparation help you succeed?

I knew it was time to move on from what I was doing. It started with a feeling, and I have always trusted my instincts. I didn't know what I was doing at the time. But I thought if I like these things I am making, others will, too. Before opening the store, I did a lot of reading and observing, speaking with people who ran stores. I didn't want to tip my hand or anything. I didn't have it all laid out. It has grown and gotten better. There's only so much preparation you can really do. I have lived in New York since 1978, and I felt I knew it very well. I had never had my own shop, but I had kept an eye on what goes on. Reading and living here—I was doing preparation all the time without realizing it.

What do you tell people who ask you for your advice?

If you don't want to do what you are currently doing, do everything you can to take the leap. Don't be afraid. It's OK to be a little nervous. Don't let your fear hold you back. As Karl Wallenda, founder of the Flying Wallendas troupe, said "Life is being on the wire; everything else is just waiting." You can have the whole safety net there, I suppose, but that would take the challenge out of it. I was single when I went to work for myself. That is a whole different situation. There is always something you can fall back on as an excuse.

What books or resources did you use or recommend others to use?

There was no book per se. The only book that sticks with me is the founder of Starbucks Howard Schultz's book *Pour Your Heart into It: How Starbucks Built a Company One Cup at a Time*. I always loved that book. *The Winner Within: A Life Plan for Team Players* by the basketball coach Pat Riley. I didn't go out and try to find a how-to book on what to do. Maybe that's because I was trying to open a shop and a gallery that didn't exist anywhere.

What are some of the surprises and unexpected rewards?

It has been this community that has come about made up of baseball lovers of all races, all types, and all ages—a great cross-section of America. The only thing they have common is baseball. They can be twenty. They can be ninety. They can be famous or someone who can't afford to buy anything. That has been the biggest surprise and satisfaction all in one. That wasn't my game plan, but that's kind of what it has turned into. You can't plan for everything, and that is really where the most fun is.

Putting Yourself Out There

Jay Goldberg advises people not to be afraid about making a leap, adding that a little nerves are OK. I couldn't agree more! I would encourage you to embrace your fears, as the people you have met on these pages have done, with grace and panache. There are lots of ways to do that. Career coaches, me included, often suggest people journal about what they are afraid of to bring it out into the open.

I also recommend that those who seek a change do at least one thing every day that they're afraid to do. It can be simple, like making a networking phone call you've been putting off or setting a coffee date. Career coach Patricia DiVecchio of International Purpose, based in Arlington, Virginia, calls this practice "building your risk muscle." So go ahead and flex that muscle.

EXPERT ADVICE ||||||||||||||||||||||||||||||||||||||||||||||||||||||||||

Beverly Jones, Career Coach

Beverly Jones offers advice with the unique position of one who's been there. In 1999, after more than two decades as a high-powered corporate lawyer, she took a golden parachute retirement package from her position as vice president of external affairs and policy at Consolidated Natural Gas. She was fifty-three.

At that age, Jones's working days were far from over. But she was ready for a break. In fact, she was eager for the respite after spending twenty-two years in a fast-paced legal career and paying her own way through a journalism degree and an MBA from Ohio University, followed by a Georgetown University law degree. "I desperately needed to recharge and map out my future," Jones says. "I had taken maybe two three-week vacations in my life. I knew now was the time to pause."

The prospect of going back to a full-time employer was daunting. "All I could think was that I'm no longer young and cute. All of a sudden I'm fifty-three and retired. I'm old. I was worried people wouldn't hire me at that age," she recalls.

When the scary notion of going to a Washington cocktail party without a good answer to the ubiquitous question, "What do you do?" arose, Jones quickly had a business card made up to hand out. It simply read: counselor, consultant, coach. "I didn't know that coaching was an established career, but it sounded good."

She passed the cards out that night, and the phone started ringing. "People wanted me!" she remembers with a laugh. Soon, people who had worked for her over the years began lining up at her door. "I had clients before I even knew what coaching was."

But it wasn't that surprising. It was the kind of attorney and boss she was. Jones's philosophy of managing had always involved trying to help people figure out their goals and ways to get there.

Jones had finally found her passion—mentoring others—even though she'd been practicing that her entire career. This time she took it on full-time and launched her own coaching/consulting practice: Clearways Consulting based in Washington, DC. "Retiring with a modest pension gave me a little flexibility," she says.

Initially, she remained loosely associated with a law firm and did a little lobbying for a nonprofit. She began to study and obtained a certificate in Leadership Coaching from Georgetown University. She attended workshops, hired her own career coach, and read extensively about the field and related areas such as self-help, spirituality, and fitness. "In time, I began to find my own voice as a coach and felt confident I was doing what I was meant to do," Jones says.

Among her current clients are attorneys, lobbyists, business owners, and executives. "Many are accomplished professionals, boomers nearing retirement—they all want to bring a new direction to their careers," says Jones.

Her own experience of switching jobs at midlife gives her the chops to back up what she preaches. "After building my own business for a decade, I know that age is not a limitation or a barrier."

||||||||||

BEVERLY'S GUIDE TO FINDING YOUR PASSION

- *Find a place to start.* You don't need a precise definition before you get going. Start by making a list of what you know you want in the next phase of your career. There is no perfect path or ideal starting point. What matters is that you somehow get moving in the general direction of where you want to go. This might be simply making a phone call to someone who works in a field that appeals to you.

- *Don't ruin your hobby.* I love to garden. When I was thinking about what to do next I thought about being a landscape designer. But I quickly realized that I'd get lonely in the garden all day—I much prefer working with people. Gardening is a great hobby and escape from work, but it wouldn't be the right career move for me. Make sure you think hard about how your passion will become a new career.

- *Stop your inner enemy.* If you have a negative refrain that goes through your head and sabotages your efforts to make a change—"I'm too old to do that"—make note of it. Write that thought down in a notebook and reframe it with a positive thought, such as, "I have these specific skills, and I'm going to use them in a new career." You need to get rid of that old blocking message to move forward with your dreams.

- *Ask the basic questions.* Does your second act fit your lifestyle? Can you afford it? What does your partner think? Ask yourself how a certain career will work with your social patterns, your spending habits, and your family situation. It will help you to dig deeper and get a clearer picture of what you truly want in your life and your options to get there.

- *Start a journal.* Journaling is a great way to map your new career direction. Make lists: the best times in your life, the things you really like, the experiences you've enjoyed, what you've excelled at, the best moments in your current career. These lists will help you home in on your passion and visualize yourself harnessing it to pursue something new and exciting.

- *Get a business card.* Want to be an artist but still working as a lawyer? Get an artist's card. As soon as you have a card, it makes the career real. You can get your second act card long before you finish your first act. I immediately got cards that said counselor, consultant, and coach— simply because I couldn't bear the thought of going to a party without a business card. I passed them out, and by the end of the evening, I *was* a coach. Printing your new information on a card can be transformative.

|||||||||||

CONNECTING WITH A CAREER COACH

If you know you need a change but are unsure of what to do, a career coach can help you set goals, clearly outline the steps to take you there, and motivate you to make it happen. I have personally used a coach to give me the kind of unbiased help a friend or family member couldn't. I found her through my dog. She and I met when training our puppies a few years ago. While serendipity allowed me to meet my career coach, asking friends for recommendations is a good place to start. You can also do research online, where you'll find a slew of directories.

Hiring the right person to guide you along on this personal journey is not simple and takes legwork. There are countless career coaches touting their services with a variety of styles and philosophies, and winnowing down the field requires doing some due diligence. The Life Planning Network (life planningnetwork.org) and 2 Young 2 Retire (2young2retire .com) offer coach directories geared to midlife workers. I recommend both sites. Also you might want to tap into expert mentor advice via PivotPlanet (pivotplanet.com); see "Meet Your Virtual Mentor" on page 12 for more information.

Here are some smart ways to find a coach who is qualified:

- *Look for qualifications.* Career coaching is a self-regulated industry and emerging profession. Many coaches have been doing it for years without adding professional designations. But designations are a sign of some formal training and of adherence to general standards of professionalism. A good place to find a directory of coaches is the International Coach Federation (coachfederation .org). The organization awards a global credential, which is currently held by thousands of coaches worldwide. ICF-credentialed coaches have met educational requirements, received specific coach training, and achieved a designated number of experience hours, among other requirements. Two other helpful sites are the Association of Career Professionals International (acpinternational .org) and the National Career Development Association (ncda.org).

- *Explore the past career path of a potential coach.* Many so-called career coaches are more life coaches, who focus on esoteric life choices and may lack practical work world advice. Find out as much as you can about their career path, both in the coaching field and in the regular work world. It's even better if they have been through a career transition or have a track record of working with people going through the process. Don't be bashful about questioning potential coaches on their level of expertise for your particular needs.

- *Ask for at least three references.* Of course, no one is going to hand over the names of clients who didn't love them, but asking for references is an important step in your process. You never know what you might learn when you get someone on the phone. Plus it's imperative to know a potential coach's work style and how he or she succeeded with other clients starting a new career.

- *Say no to group sessions.* Find a coach who conducts one-on-one sessions. These can be in person, by phone, or by Skype, by Google+ Hangout, or by email, but you want his or her full attention. Phone sessions are commonplace these days, which in many ways is to your advantage. You aren't restricted to signing on with a coach in your town, and you don't waste time getting to and from meetings and making small talk.

- *Expect a free initial consultation.* Once you've narrowed your search, you'll want to interview a few candidates. Never agree to work with a coach without a trial run. This initial session should be gratis. If there is a charge for this meet and greet, pass.

- *Ask about fees.* Rates vary significantly, anywhere from $50 to more than $200 per hour. Some coaches require a minimum number of hours. On average, coach–client relationships last from six months to a year. You might sign on for one or two meetings to jump-start your new career course, or weekly or monthly meetings might suit your needs better. Some coaches will provide resources such as books and give homework assignments to prepare for future sessions.

- *Check out the coach's website.* This should give you insight into the coach's areas of expertise and what he or she has published. Search the coach's name on the web and see if you find uncensored comments written by other clients. You can find coaches who have a blog via directories such as Alltop.com (search under "career") or who are on Twitter by searching WeFollow under #coach.

- *Get a written agreement.* This is a business relationship, so treat it like one with a formal agreement that defines the duties of each party. Verbal agreements can be risky and leave both the client and the coach susceptible to unexpected misunderstandings.

By working through these steps, you have a good chance of hiring a reputable coach. But there is one more thing. It comes down to something intangible—a human connection. You'll be doling out private details of your life, your dreams, your strengths and weaknesses with your coach. You have to trust the coach and feel comfortable laying it all before him or her. This is scary stuff, and you need a steady hand to hold from time to time.

Ultimately, the career coach you hire should inspire you, push you, and give you the inner confidence to step into the unfamiliar with the grace and strength that comes from knowing deep inside that you are on the right path.

Keep in mind that if you're unemployed, your local unemployment office may be able to set you up with free career counseling. Look for library, community colleges, and the alumni offices of your alma mater for coaching sessions and workshops. CareerOneStop (careeronestop.org), sponsored by the Department of Labor, offers coaching and special programs for military members moving into the private sector at various locations around the country. These could be small groups, but helpful nonetheless to get you moving forward.

CHAPTER ELEVEN

Stitching Together a New Life

Susan Wolcott is a child of the sixties. As soon as she graduated from high school in 1969, she left her hometown of Olympia, Washington, and "did the hippie thing," she says, taking the time to find out what was important to her—community, listening, spirituality, holistic health, creativity, the environment.

She found a profession that reflected those values—nursing. It felt right. "Nursing to me meant kindness and compassion for human beings," says Wolcott. For twelve years, she worked as a clinical nurse in hospices, home care, hospitals, and rehabilitation and outpatient clinics. Eventually, she moved into higher-paying managerial positions at managed-care companies and software firms specializing in healthcare.

But as healthcare began to be driven more by insurance and less by patient care, Wolcott became disillusioned. She kept her day job but went back to school, earning a master's degree in social and organizational learning from George Mason University in Fairfax, Virginia, where she had relocated with four adopted children after her divorce. In 2002, she started moonlighting as a life coach, helping people deal with personal and professional transitions. While coaching others, she realized she needed to make some changes of her own.

"My earliest memory is the peaceful sound of my mother's knitting needles clicking together," says Wolcott, who began knitting at nine. She had recently picked the needles up again, after a sixteen-year hiatus, during a weekend in Santa Fe with her mother and two sisters. "I soon found that in a tense or tired moment, knitting a few rows brought me back to calmness and centeredness," she says.

Before long, she and her sister Jill, an avid knitter and knitwear designer in San Francisco, had started a side business called Y2Knit, a series of teaching retreats. It hit the market just as the knitting boom was taking off. According to the Craft Yarn Council of America, the number of women ages forty-five and younger who knit regularly has doubled since 1998, to almost one in five. "Knitting relaxes people by giving them something to focus on," Wolcott says. As their workshop business grew, Jill began designing patterns for Y2Knit to sell.

Meanwhile, scoping out a location for a retreat, Wolcott drove through the rolling Maryland farmland seventy miles northwest of Washington, DC, and sensed that this could be home.

It was then she decided to quit her job as a director with an online physician–patient communications network and buy a place in the country. It would be both home and yarn store. "It hit me with a total assurance," she recalls. She was over fifty and felt a "deepening of this desire to do something that was meaningful and purposeful."

She eventually landed in quaint Funkstown, Maryland, as the owner of a, well, funky, pink log house dating back to 1780. In the summer of 2003, Wolcott opened the brightly painted Y2Knit retail shop.

She grew the profitable business to an active client list of five thousand, and Wolcott covered her rent and living expenses, though she earned only about a quarter of her last job's pay. "My change was about lifestyle," she says.

She has become her own boss, operates in a creative world, and buys much of her food from local farmers. She has no commute to work. Her fifteen-year-old Honda is usually parked in the driveway.

More important, the entrepreneurial venture has reconnected Wolcott with the altruistic values that had originally led her to nursing. "I have a ministry," she says. "Not in a religious way, but it's about ministering to people and meeting their needs." Connecting people with resources fills her days. Women stop by to talk about kids, spouses, recipes, job interviews, movies, dreams, and frustrations.

"I have no regrets about giving up the paycheck," Wolcott says. "My life is not about money—it's about my spirit."

Author's Note: Susan is now the owner of Yarnability/Sewinclined in Shepherdstown, West Virginia.

I asked Susan to look back and share her thoughts on her transition to the small business world.

What did the transition mean to you personally?

It was about being really true to what I believe. As we go through life, we often make choices that are best because our parents want us to, or because society wants us to, or because it's best for our children. Those aren't wrong choices necessarily, but they are the things that impact our choices. This was a chance for me to make choices totally based on what my soul wanted.

Were you confident that you were doing the right thing? Any second-guessing?

I didn't have a lot of second-guessing. Sometimes I'd wake up and think, What the heck am I doing? But I really didn't have doubts. It felt very much like this was totally going to work out. Once I'd moved, I realized I was living in a very conservative, Bible Belt area, which was a little challenging for me because that is not who I am. There were times when I would meditate for two hours in the morning, focusing on affirmations.

Now all it takes is a couple quick words to myself to know that this is going to turn out OK.

Anything you would have done differently?

I don't know that I can go there. There is nothing big that sticks out in my mind.

How do you measure your success?

I do have measurements. They are not crystal clear all the time. One of them is, Do I get out of bed in the morning and look forward to the day ahead? I think we all have had that experience.

Part of the success that I measure is the incredible interactions with people, and I have them several times a week, where I see some kind of transformation in them. It could be as simple as, oh, they now get their knitting project. More often, it is something deeper within their lives that somehow has happened as a result of that project, a little aha moment. Very often they say, "I am so glad you are here." And that's how I measure my success.

And certainly the fact that I pay the rent and bills every month.

How big a role did financial rewards play in your decision to make a transition?

It is not a part of it. It was never about the money.

How did your preparation help you succeed?

I took it slowly. My preparation had a lot to do with building up my inner resources and developing a strong sense of self. I kept doing positive affirmations. They helped me prepare and still do.

And then having an external support system is key. I have that. My children are supportive. My mother, who is eighty-six, is very supportive, and so are my friends.

My education also helped build my confidence. My graduate degree in social and organizational behavior added to my tool kit. I am probably overeducated for what I am doing, or some people might perceive that. But I couldn't do what I am doing without that added education. It gave me a stronger sense of self, really empowered me.

At the same time, it also provided me with the technical knowledge about business organization, how to run a meeting professionally, and how to write a great business plan. As I work within this industry, it really helps to have that grounding, it continually helps me as I create and grow the business.

Coaching was also a focus of my education and preparation for this new stage. I studied with the Coaches Training Institute and co-taught a class after graduation in group dynamics. Today, I coach formally, as well as pretty much all the time with people; even teaching knitting is like coaching somebody. So I feel like I gained some really wonderful skills there that have made me a really great teacher.

What do you tell people who ask for your advice?

I tell them that if it is burning in you, in my belief, you absolutely need to follow it. You're not serving yourself, or anybody, if you don't.

I think you do have to make sure there is water in the pool and that it is deep enough. You can't just jump off the end of the dock. You can't abandon everything and jump into a new field without some preparation. It may mean a transition period where you need to build up financial security or learn a new skill set, but you can certainly start trying to figure it out and take small steps.

Don't start a small business without a clear, solid business plan. Make sure that it's a *written* business plan. It is really important to write these things down, so they are not just ideas in your head. Know what you are going to do. Have "what if" scenarios. What if you don't make as much money as you think you're going to do?

Our plan is a comprehensive one. First, we have several lines of business. I think the reason we have succeeded is it is not just the store—it's also the line of patterns and events. We have a combination of things.

Second, part of our business plan is a strong marketing approach. You have to know how you are going to sell your product and services. Our website is a big part of that. If you don't have a website, no one is going to take you seriously. You can create the website yourself or you can pay somebody to do it. You need to keep it current, though. We just redid our website to better reflect us.

Once you know where you are heading, review the plan at set intervals. Jill and I got together a few weeks ago because our plan had some holes in it. It had weakened. It's really easy to start using bubble gum to patch up the holes—but we needed to reevaluate the way we were doing things.

It's important to network with people in the field you are entering. We are very active in our trade association. Even though we are a small business with two people, we make the time. We're both on Twitter! Jill has more followers than I do. I said, "I'm not going there . . . it's just one more thing . . ." I resisted. I have to force myself to stay up with the new technology and social networking.

I tell people to seek out a career coach and not just because I studied it. I think it's a good idea for many people going through a career change. Coaching is like therapy. There are times when you need it. There's nothing wrong with it. I invite people who are interested in starting a knit shop to come for a personal retreat here, to come spend a day.

What books or resources did you use or recommend others to use?

Cheryl Richardson's *Life Makeovers* and *Take Time for Your Life*, and Barbara Sher's *I Could Do Anything If I Only Knew What It Was*.

> "I have no regrets about giving up the paycheck. My life is not about money—it's about my spirit."

What are some of the biggest surprises and unexpected rewards?

The wonderful people I've met and discovered and then the wellspring within myself that has come out. People who have known me throughout my entire life would say I am a strong person. That has manifested itself in new ways in this career. I almost hate to say it because I find it really trite, but this is where I am supposed to be.

PREPARE YOURSELF

The secret to a successful second career begins with knowing who you are and where your talents will shine. Many of us know we want and need to keep working. Yet we're a little unsure of what work we're best suited to do. Finding the best job can be a soul-searching undertaking.

If you're not sure where you want to go, it's OK. Pause and allow yourself the time to make a frank evaluation of your skills and interests. Much of what you already know is transferable to your next pursuit, but it will take some self-exploration to see what truly suits you and your background.

The key is to match your job or career to your interests and personality.

A good career coach can help you drill down, as can worksheets found in books like *The Encore Career Handbook: How to Make a Living and a Difference in the Second Half of Life* by Marci Alboher. There are also simple free self-assessment quizzes online—for example, at CareerPath.com and Monster (monster.com). Career assessment tests rank among the most popular methods used to research a new job (in addition to exploring websites and consulting with friends and family, former coworkers, and others in the industry).

These career assessment tools provide a broad view of your interests, abilities, and personal values—all of which play an integral role in job choices and, ultimately, your job satisfaction. Gaining an awareness of occupational and personal temperaments, study habits, and job values can lead to meaningful and informed decision making. The expectation, of course, is that the results open up a variety of options to explore for a career shift and give you important insight into your working style to help you find the best fit.

Two things to keep in mind:

- Don't expect a career assessment to point you to your future job per se. The results are merely suggestions based on that one area of assessment.

- Give honest answers. If you consciously or subconsciously answer questions to fit a preconceived outcome you have in mind, the results will not be very useful.

Write a Business Plan

More and more workers are exiting the once-secure realm of corporate jobs—many because of layoffs—and starting their own businesses. Last year, more than six hundred thousand small firms were started in the United States, according to the Small Business Administration. Trouble is, only half will survive beyond five years.

It takes far more than a brilliant idea to succeed. A business plan can help you get organized, not to mention, you'll want one when it comes time to secure a loan, financing, or local support. You and your business plan can land among the winners if you do the prep work. You may have to study marketing, finance, and employment law. But don't be turned off by that. There's plenty of information, both online and in books, to help you on your path. If you're looking for more personal guidance, sign up for a community college or certification program to get the necessary skills. You can begin by contacting your town's or county's Small Business Development Center. A three-hour course in the essentials of starting a business or email marketing might cost as little as $15 to $30.

There's no strict model to follow, but in general, a simple plan— which you'll have to submit to get a loan or other financing—should be about twenty pages. Your plan should first include an executive summary, which explains what your company will do, who the customers will be, why you are qualified to run it, how you'll sell your goods and services, and your financial outlook. A detailed description of the business, its location, who your management team is, and what your staffing requirements are should follow. You'll also want to include information about your industry and competition. How does your idea cater to a need in the marketplace? What's truly different about your product, your service, your approach?

A separate section should be devoted to market analysis. This part targets your customers more specifically, including age, gender, and where they live. The analysis also will describe your sales and promotional strategy to reach them. How big is the potential market? Finally, you should include a realistic forecast of start-up outlays—cost of raw materials, equipment, employee salaries, marketing materials, insurance, utilities, and fees for attorneys and accountants—and how much you expect to sell and to earn.

CHAPTER TWELVE

Learning Life's Lessons

On the day of his ex-business partner's funeral, Cliff Stevenson found a flier stuck in his door. It was an ad for a teaching degree at a nearby college. And it struck a nerve.

Stevenson had harbored a desire to teach since his undergraduate days at the University of Pennsylvania. But when he saw only a handful of upperclassmen getting teaching jobs, he dropped the master of education program he'd been eyeing and earned bachelor's degrees in economics and history. Later, he returned to Penn for an MBA from Wharton. In 1981, a job in real-estate finance and mortgage banking landed him a lucrative career in Pittsburgh.

Just two weeks before the funeral in 1996, Stevenson's dying partner had asked: "So what are you going to do with your life, Stevo? You said you weren't going to do this mortgage thing forever."

For Stevenson, fifty-five, that early death, combined with the sudden death of his brother at age forty-three not long before, was a life-changing event. "You never know what's going to happen in life," he says. "I knew it was the right time to do something different."

So he chucked his twenty-year career to follow his heart. Stevenson now teaches social studies to eighth graders and high school students in the Hampton Township School District in Allison Park, outside Pittsburgh. His salary is about one-sixth of what he made in his best years as a mortgage banker. "I didn't want to turn seventy-five and ask, What did I do with my life? I financed and sold real estate," says Stevenson. "I want to give back, to have an effect on somebody."

Self-confident and disciplined, Stevenson also benefited from the full support of his wife, Diane, who earns a solid income as a regional merchandise manager for Macy's. The couple has no children. They sold their century-old Victorian home outside Pittsburgh for twice what they paid, downsizing to a smaller townhouse on up-and-coming Washington's Landing, an island in the Allegheny River, within spitting distance of Pittsburgh's downtown Golden Triangle. Now they don't have a mortgage.

Next, Stevenson went back to school. For two years before he resigned from his firm, he took night courses to get a master's degree in education at Duquesne University. Because he had an undergraduate degree in history, all he needed were seven additional courses in education to be certified as a social studies teacher in Pennsylvania.

That said, he still had to wait for a job to open. His first year was spent working a $5,000-stipend internship in a local school district, followed by another two years as a substitute teacher. Then he was hired at Hampton.

In many ways, his twenty years of corporate deal making gives Stevenson an edge. He's teaching his students skills they need for life—how to write effectively, speak confidently in public, and solve problems under pressure.

It's surprising that he works more hours than he did in his old career; arriving at school by 7 a.m., he shuttles between two schools, where he teaches a total of four courses per day and 158 students. He wraps up his workday around 6:30. He goes home, cooks dinner, and heads upstairs to his office for a couple of hours of grading papers and preparing for the next day's classes.

The payback is a passion for his work, a better night's sleep, and improved health. Stevenson also feels intellectually stimulated by teaching timely topics and current affairs. And, of course, the feedback he gets from his pupils can't be measured: "I'm always amazed when a student emails me from college, thanking me for pushing him or her to do their best. You never know when you've touched someone."

I asked Cliff to look back and share his thoughts on his transition to the world of teaching.

What did the transition mean to you personally?

I came to Pittsburgh when I was thirty years old. I was hired by a mortgage banking company here, and it required a lot of selling. I'm not really a cold-call seller. I saw myself doing that for ten years but no more.

When I got to be forty, I realized I was halfway through my life, and I thought, OK, what have I done? We didn't have kids. My wife had a decent job, and we're not very materialistic. The need for money was not the issue. I knew we would always be able to feed ourselves and cover our medical bills.

I tell my seniors the last day of class about the triangle of life— body, mind, and soul. You have to keep those things in balance.

I realized that there has got to be more to life than just going to work and bringing home good money, buying nice stuff. Before you die, you want to be able to say you made a difference—maybe not to the world, but in somebody else's life.

Were you confident that you were doing the right thing? Any second-guessing?

I didn't have any second-guessing about becoming a teacher. I did second-guess about my ability to get a job.

Anything you would have done differently?

I don't think so.

How do you measure your success?

I ask myself, "Do I feel good about it?" And I do. The kids tell me they're glad they had me for a teacher. Parents come up to me and thank me. I would be worried if I weren't getting that kind of feedback. It makes me think I am doing it the right way.

How big a role did financial rewards play in your decision to make a transition?

None. I've been teaching full-time for seven years now. When we bought this condo, we put on a minimum mortgage to get some tax write-off. When you don't have big mortgages or credit card debt or car loans, you can live on far less income.

How did your preparation help you succeed?

I started planning years before I switched careers. My wife and I thought carefully about the financial aspects. When I decided I wanted to make this move, I set a target date for when I would leave my mortgage banking business. That allowed me to go to school at night on the sly and pick up my education degree over a two-year period. I would take a course a semester, while continuing to work for two full years, trying to stuff away as much money as I could.

I left when I was forty-four. I figured if I waited too long, I would get to the point where I was too old.

I was also patient. I was able to pave my way through the internship program that exists for teachers in Pennsylvania. It's a one-year internship in which you work for a school, and they pay you $5,000, using you as a sub. I did that for a year and continued to sub for another two years. Then when Hampton hired me, I worked half-time for two years.

I made a backup plan. As I was going to get my education degree, I was also taking classes to become a financial planner in case I couldn't find work as a teacher. I have an MBA in finance from Wharton, so I knew about money management. To be a planner, you have to take five specific courses on taxes and insurance to be nationally certified.

We downsized and simplified our lives. We wanted to change our lifestyle and get reinvigorated. We loved our house, but it was a hundred-year-old house with an acre of land. Every weekend there were four or five chores to be done. I like to do that stuff myself, but it was too much. Moving to the two-bedroom condo freed up a lot of time.

What do you tell people who ask for your advice?

Think about what you enjoy and what you might want to do ahead of time. I began by taking a half-day class at a community college that cost $40. It was a chance to spend time evaluating myself through a self-analysis course designed to identify my abilities, values, and interests. You take the tests over three hours and then graph the results together. Where they intersect, you find careers you might consider. It got me thinking. Do you want to work alone or with people? Flexible hours or set ones?

Don't worry if you don't know immediately what it is you want to do in your next career. Initially, I hadn't thought about teaching. I thought I would need to take far too many courses to get accredited. Then I found out that in Pennsylvania, with my economic and history degree, I only had to take seven specific courses mandated by the state. It wasn't until I got that brochure in the mail the day of the funeral that the light went on. I don't know if I would have ever thought about it.

Be a good Boy Scout, be prepared. Think hard about the financial aspects. Make sure you have the support of your spouse or partner. Have a plan, a timetable. I was clear: I'm going to go to school at night. I'm going to cover seven courses in two years. I had a backup plan, to be a financial planner if it didn't work out. And I knew I would have to sub for a period of time.

> "I didn't want to get to seventy-five and turn around and ask, What did I do with my life?"

Be pragmatic. It's good to have a passion—mine might have been to play Major League Baseball—but that's never going to happen! You have to do what your abilities and your personality are. You have to be honest with yourself. Know your strengths and weaknesses. Take the time to analyze yourself. Do the self-reflection. I am a very reflective person.

I'm not a risk taker. I'm a calculated risk taker.

What books or resources did you use or recommend others to use?

Read *Zen and the Art of Making a Living*. It's a self-analysis book about finding what is meaningful to you and what you really want to do.

What are some of the surprises and unexpected rewards?

The thing I like about teaching is you can never be good enough. You can always be better. It is challenging and always will be. The most positive thing I get is the feedback from the kids. I get letters from kids the year after they graduate, saying "I want to thank you. Your class was the most collegelike class I took in high school. You were tough, but I'm glad I had you." That's what's in it for me.

WAYS TO GET IN FINANCIAL SHAPE
TO MAKE IT WORK

Downsizing your home and being mortgage-free like Cliff Stevenson was able to do while moving forward to a new career that pays less at least initially may not be an option for you. And not everyone lives in a neighborhood where refinancing a mortgage is an option. Even picking up stakes and moving to a less expensive place to live and work is not an easy choice for many career changers. But all of these are worth exploring because your living costs are usually the biggest nut to cut in your monthly budget.

There are, however, plenty of ways you can creatively trim your lifestyle to make the necessary budget cuts. The following small and large actions can give you the cushion that will make you nimble enough to take a chance on your second act without worrying about making ends meet. There is nothing better than financial planning well ahead of time. I'm a big believer in having an emergency fund of a year's living expenses set aside to ease your transition, but this may not be a realistic option for many of you.

There's also a possibility that you may have received a lump-sum retirement package from an ex-employer if you decided to step up and accept their offer and step out. In that scenario, you might continue to draw a salary for a year or more, that's your golden nugget. If you have spouse or a partner who can carry the water for a time, that too, can ease the financial risk of jumping into a new career.

And if you're thinking ahead about your next act, the following are ways you can take your life into your own hands today through smart money management:

- *Track your spending.* This is not a new technique, but it works. Take a small notebook and pen everywhere you go and jot down everything you spend money on for a week, a month if you have the discipline. It may surprise you how easy it is to find the frivolous expenses that can add up.

- *Note the minutiae.* There are dozens of mindless ways money can slip through your hands—from a latté at the local coffee shop, a can of soda at work, or the *People* magazine bought impulsively at the supermarket checkout counter.

- *Contain the change.* You should grow keenly aware of the times you just shove the change from a purchase in your pocket or drop it to the bottom of your purse. There it floats indefinitely around in a vacuum, maybe even falling down between your car seats, lost in the upholstered underworld.

- *Save all receipts*, even the smallest one from a tin of breath mints. Scrutinize your bills. You'll discover there are two types of monthly expenses. There are fixed expenses that you are obligated to pay each month, no matter what (for example, your mortgage or rent, student loan payments, car payments, cable/satellite TV, or electric bill). If you pay a fixed expense on a quarterly basis, your car insurance for example, then determine how much that averages out to on a monthly basis. The other kind of expenses are variable expenses, those that change each month (such as your dry cleaning bills, transportation expenses, or the amount you spend eating out). Your expenses that change each month will be the easiest to get control over fast.

- Your checking account records and credit card receipts should let you see where you've splurged on haircuts or highlighting, vacations, meals out, magazine subscriptions, movies, and gifts. You can start cutting back on those costs immediately. You'll have to be rigorous, but keep your eyes on the prize.

CHAPTER THIRTEEN

From High Finance to Ravioli

It's a sunny Sunday in September, and Tim Sheerer is not on the golf course with his fifteen-year-old son, Johnny, playing in the annual father–son tournament. Instead, he's spending the day preparing meals for roughly 350 customers at La Cappella, an Italian bistro, in a Pittsburgh suburb. That's the restaurant he owns and operates with his wife, Colleen. The cook has called in sick.

Sheerer, forty-seven, is OK with that. Missing the golf outing is disappointing, but it's a rarity. In the six years since he traded in a $500,000-a-year Wall Street salary to start his own restaurant, he has spent many hours with his four kids, ages thirteen to nineteen, at various sporting events.

After graduating with an MBA from the University of Chicago, Sheerer spent over thirteen years rising through the ranks of Merrill Lynch's U.S. Money Market Group, specializing in short-term corporate debt. He worked a crazy schedule—one day London, the next

Milwaukee. Colleen was in charge of the kids and hugged the side-lines at their games. "I wasn't able to be there for them," Sheerer says.

Sports and family mean a lot to Sheerer. But he pressed on year after year for one more whopping January bonus—skipping the BMW, sailboat, and second home. In time, he saved enough to leave investment banking and head to Pittsburgh, his hometown.

The idea to move back home started to take shape in the spring of 2001 when Sheerer's father, who had nearly died from a heart attack some sixteen years earlier, underwent quadruple bypass surgery. When Sheerer turned forty shortly after the September 11 attacks, it was a turning point for him. "I looked around, and I wanted more," he says. He asked himself what meant most to him. The answer was simple: family.

Although the Sheerers belonged to a gourmet-cooking club, the notion of operating their own Italian restaurant never crossed their minds. It just worked out that way. Sheerer's sister knew of a new restaurant franchise venture moving into the Pittsburgh area. Intrigued, Sheerer signed on and eventually leased retail space. He spent a year working in one of the chain's existing suburban restaurants. He bused tables, washed dishes, sautéed, and more. "If I was going to ask someone else to do these jobs, I had to know how to do them myself," he says. Ultimately, Sheerer extricated himself from the franchise operator, opted to open an independent restaurant, and named it La Cappella, or the Chapel, for the Fox Chapel community many of its customers live in.

Sheerer's energetic entrepreneurial spirit and business and finance background, combined with his wife's people skills, have made the effort rewarding. Restaurant regulars call Colleen the "ambassador" of the cozy, 110-seat dining establishment, which is tucked alongside a heavily trafficked strip mall. Three of the couple's kids work as busers, hosts, and waiters. It's a family affair.

Although eighty-hour weeks were standard early on for Sheerer, today the schedule is not so demanding. If one of the kids has a game, he will be there, oftentimes coaching. With four college tuitions in sight, La Cappella will have to show more of a profit in time. But for now, with a lower cost of living, no mortgage payment, and savings to tap, the couple has a cushion.

Until his death in 2013, Sheerer's dad was also able to see almost every one of his grandchildren's games since the family moved to Pittsburgh. "You can't put a price on that," says Sheerer.

"And then we look at our children," says Colleen. "They're happy and thriving." Sheerer nods in agreement. "They're our legacy. We made this move for them and their future," he says, as he heads back to the kitchen.

I asked Tim to look back and share his thoughts on his transition to a restaurateur.

What did the transition mean to you personally?

A couple things happened. As a result of 9/11, I felt a major loss. I saw people I worked with pass away. In the Merrill Lynch grind, you go through every day, and you work, work, work, but that made me realize, hey, you only live once.

That combined with my dad's bypass surgery, got us thinking about a change. When Colleen and I moved to New York, we thought we would only be there for five years, but we never reevaluated it.

When we did really sit down and say, we're making a lot of money, but is this really where we want to be? Is this really what we want to do? Is this where we want the kids to grow up? If we don't talk about it now, ten years will go by like that, and we're passed the point where we can really consider a move.

I was working a zillion hours, and I was starting to miss things with the kids that my brothers in Pittsburgh were able to do. My brother complained he wasn't making enough money, but he was coaching all his kids' sports teams. I couldn't even see my daughter play in a softball game because I was either out of town or still in the office.

Were you confident that you were doing the right thing? Any second-guessing?

I was going into a big unknown. I definitely second-guessed it— more often at two in the morning, when I was lying awake in bed. When you are plowing through the day, there is really no time for second-guessing. But when you wake up in the middle of the night, that's when you ask, Is this the right move?

Anything you would have done differently?

I would have taken more time. Initially, I was a franchisee, part of a chain of Italian restaurants. I was anxious to get going. I was energized. I wanted it badly. I needed to slow down and do my due diligence. I just kept saying, yeah, this is perfect for me.

I needed to trust my gut. I relied on the franchise experts to tell me about certain things. At that point, I was not an authority on the restaurant business, so I trusted their advice. At the same time, though, there were four or five things about the design of the restaurant and purveyors that my gut told me to do differently.

But going the franchise route gave me enough confidence that I could get into the restaurant business successfully. I don't think I would have been comfortable leaving Merrill Lynch and opening up my own ma-and-pa restaurant without that interim move. I would have thought it was too big of a step. And as a result, when I opened my own restaurant, I was better prepared.

How do you measure your success?

I had a boss who measured his success by how much Merrill would pay him, how many cars he had, how many homes he had. That's not how I measure my success. Mine's measured by my kids. I look to my kids every day. I've had to do that the last five years while the restaurant isn't making nearly the amount of money I want it to and certainly not what I made on Wall Street.

Are our kids happy? Are they successful? Are they getting opportunities? I think society today is way too materialistic. It is nice to aspire to make money, and it is nice to aspire to have nice things. We had a huge home and a huge kitchen with a Viking refrigerator—but if you don't have your family, you're lost.

I did a lot of multimillion-dollar deals when I worked on Wall Street. I had a lot of fun. But the thing I have been most successful at is coaching a basketball team that I now have time to do. We're 18–0 this year. I think I am teaching these kids how to be successful, how to compete, what you can accomplish with hard work.

How big a role did financial rewards play in your decision to make a transition?

None. In fact, it was the opposite. I think in some cases, people have a job and make a career change because they want to make more money or need to make more money. For me, the money was good at Merrill Lynch, but the other aspects of the job weren't. I had done it for a long time, and I wasn't getting the reward out of the job that I used to get. In fact, I was getting kind of cynical about it because I was missing opportunities to do things with my family and my kids.

I moved to this new career knowing upfront that I wouldn't be able to make anywhere near the amount of money I used to make. Sometimes you have to measure financial rewards versus other rewards and decide what's more important.

How did your preparation help you succeed?

Most of my preparation was on-the-ground training. I trained for six months at another franchisee's restaurant before mine opened. I went in from 8 a.m. to 8 p.m. and did everything. I wanted to really understand what all the workers go through.

In a restaurant, a lot of owners stay out front, and they'll point at the kitchen and jokingly say, "That's my executive chef's field, I don't go back there." Not me. I can break down a dish machine. I sauté.

Last night, it was a cold, rainy Tuesday night, and we expected it to be slow, but the restaurant filled up, we had a fifteen-minute wait for tables. It was crazy. I went back in the kitchen where the executive chef and cooks were getting killed. I left Colleen up front, and I basically cooked for an hour to relieve the pressure. I can do that.

The second piece of my preparation that has been invaluable— securing the support of my family before I started. I had been successful in my first career, and the family trusted me. No one second-guessed me. The first couple of weeks in the restaurant, I was so busy, I couldn't even see straight, and I was thinking oh my god, I don't know if I can do this kind of thing. My youngest brother and my sister came in and went to work. They bartended. They bussed tables. They did it without me even asking.

What advice do you tell people who ask for your advice?

Don't jump in too fast. Do your due diligence. Take time to do what it is you want. I know it is very much a cliché, but you only live once. I say that phrase a lot to Colleen and the kids. There are too many times that you hear that people don't do something, then five, ten, fifteen years later, they regret it. You must stop and really say, what are my goals? I think most of us live our lives without goals, or at least you don't sit down and put them on paper.

I don't know too many people who write down the pros and cons of their decisions. We did. We measured all that.

What books or resources did you use or recommend others to use?

Nothing beats real life experience. Not just on-the-job training, but talking to people who have been in the business. That's your best resource. I talked to people who owned restaurants. I talked to people running sub shops, fast-food restaurants, people who had worked as servers in particular restaurants. I bought a couple of books, but until I was doing it, those didn't help me. Talk to as many people as you can to get real-life input.

> "We look at our children. They're happy and thriving. They're our legacy. We made this move for them and their future."

What are some of the surprises and unexpected rewards?

The biggest surprise was not a good one. I planned to tap into my Merrill Lynch stock options as a financial cushion when needed. I thought I was in good shape with those to help us weather the storm in the restaurant the first couple of years. Then in 2008 my investment portfolio basically dried up.

I learned it's important to go back and look at your investments. Are they safe? Obviously, in my case, the last two years they weren't safe. That was something I did not foresee and didn't contemplate. Merrill Lynch has been around forever.

We expected the restaurant part to be tough, but we didn't expect all the money we saved to disappear in one fell swoop. We wake up and look at each other and say, well, we have our health, and the kids are all healthy.

A more positive reward is having time with the kids. First, we have them helping out in the restaurant. Colleen and I love it. The kids and the workers all know each other, and the employees are involved in the kids' lives. They actually care whether Johnny hits a home run in the game. And the fun part is I get to spend a lot more time with them. If I were still on Wall Street, Molly would be going to college at Penn State this year, and I don't know how well I would know her. Now I can go shopping with her for prom dresses.

The ABCs of Franchising

For his first two years in the restaurant business, Tim Sheerer was a franchisee of an Italian restaurant chain. It taught him the ropes and gave him the confidence to make the initial change and, eventually, to embark on his own small, family-run eatery.

Not all franchises are created equal, and getting into the game can be expensive. Within the same industry, the more expensive franchises are better known in the marketplace; therefore, they can command a higher price because you are buying into the value of a well-known name. The less expensive franchises may not have any name recognition and are looking to expand their presence in the market by offering their franchises at a much lower price. It is essential that you do your homework and research on a potential franchisee to avoid future mishaps.

Careful planning is fundamental to success. The U.S. Small Business Administration (sba.gov) offers resources to help you get started. Here are some guidelines from the SBA:

- *What is franchising?* A franchise is a legal and commercial relationship between the owner of a trademark, service mark, trade name, or advertising symbol and an individual or group wishing to use that identification in a business. The franchise governs the method of conducting business between the two parties. Generally, a franchisee sells goods or services that are supplied by the franchiser or that meet the franchiser's quality standards. The franchiser provides the business expertise (marketing plans, management guidance, financing assistance, site location, training, etc.) that otherwise would not be available to the franchisee. The franchisee brings the entrepreneurial spirit and drive necessary to make the franchise a success.

- *The two forms of franchising.* Product/trade name franchising and business format franchising. In the simplest form, a franchiser owns the right to the name or trademark and sells that right to a franchisee. This is known as product/trade name franchising. The more complex form, business format franchising, involves a broader ongoing relationship between the two parties. Business format franchises, such as the one Tim Sheerer was involved with, often provide a full range of services, including site selection, training, product supply, marketing plans, and even assistance in obtaining financing.

- *Buying a franchise.* Because of the risk and work involved in starting a new business, many new entrepreneurs choose franchising as an alternative to the risk of starting a new, independent business from scratch. One of the biggest mistakes you can make is to hurry into business, as Tim Sheerer did, so it's important to understand your reasons for going into business and determine whether owning a business is right for you. But remember that hard work, commitment, and sacrifice are essential to the success of any business venture, including franchising.

BEFORE YOU DIVE INTO A FRANCHISE

The franchise business may not be booming, but it is slowly gaining ground. The number of franchise establishments in the United States is expected to increase to 757,055 units in 2013, up from 736,114 in 2011, according to the International Franchise Association. If you're interested in opening a franchise, here are some ways to avoid pitfalls and evaluate which one might be right for you:

Go slowly. One of the biggest mistakes you can make is to hurry into business, "I would have taken more time," says Sheerer, who switched careers from investment banking a decade ago. For his first two years, he was a franchisee of an Italian restaurant chain, but that foray wasn't a success for him. "I needed to slow down and do my due diligence. I just kept saying, yeah, this is perfect for me. At that point, I was not an authority on the restaurant business, so I trusted the franchisor's advice. At the same time, though, there were four or five things about the design of the restaurant and choice of purveyors that my gut told me to do differently."

Though a bit tricky in the beginning, the franchise route initially did help him learn the ropes of a new industry and gave him enough confidence that he could get into the restaurant business successfully. Visit the U.S. Small Business Administration (sba.gov) for franchising business resources to help you get your research under way.

Do a self-assessment. "People fall in love with a concept, product or service, but don't look at what skills it takes to succeed in that business," notes Jania Bailey, president of franchise-consulting firm FranNet. What are you really good at? Time management? Customer service? Networking? If you're someone who is not able to walk into a room of two hundred strangers and make two hundred new friends, perhaps a heavy sales business is not for you, she says.

Franchisors are looking for people with transferable business skills—sales, marketing, leadership, communication, and customer service skills. It's important to realize that, regardless of the sales pitch, you're not really your own boss. You don't call the shots. If that's what you want, franchising is not for you. You must follow the formula. There's little wiggle room for innovation. Franchises depend on the by-the-book execution of a business plan. In general, they want you to have a willingness to do what you're told, period. "If you aren't comfortable following a system, you have no business being in franchising," according to Bailey.

Be a detective. The franchise sector is regulated by the Federal Trade Commission (ftc.gov), which offers a consumer guide to buying a franchise with handy resources to help you avoid common scams. Step one is to request a franchisor's disclosure document. It provides contact information for previous purchasers in your region, audited financial statements, a breakdown of start-up and ongoing costs, and an outline of your responsibilities and the franchiser's obligations, among other vital background information.

If you have any questions, call the FTC hotline at 1-877-382-4357. Pay keen attention to the pages showing franchisee turnover in the document. Names and phone numbers of former and current franchisees in your area should be listed. Contacting former franchisees may take some legwork, but you want to know why they're no longer in business. You might find, for instance, that the promised training didn't materialize for them or that the robust marketing support that was touted upfront never materialized.

Interview other franchisees. Talk to franchisees at all levels of the business from those who are wildly successful to middle of the pack and those who are struggling to get a realistic view, Bailey recommends. About 25 percent knock it out of the park, 60 percent make a good living, and 20 percent struggle, she says. It's best to interview franchisees in person. Chances are they will be more forthcoming face to face. Be aware that some may have signed confidentiality agreements that prevent them from talking to you.

Have a savings cushion. How much can you afford to lose? Do you have a financial cushion to cover your living expenses for a year or more? If not, pump the brakes. It's essential to do a budget and figure how much you will need to live on while your start-up gains traction.

Be realistic. While some franchises do break even quickly, most take eighteen months or more before a newcomer can draw a salary. While the initial fee for a franchise is clearly stated in the disclosure documents, newcomers often underestimate operating costs, says Bailey. You need funds socked away for the unexpected and you should probably plan conservatively to lose money for the first two years. Chances are you will need to land a loan to cover your initial investment and start-up costs. Getting into the game can be pricey—for example, an initial investment of around $66,000 might be required for a Merry Maids unit or $1.4 million for a Panera Bread restaurant. A $200,000 to $500,000 investment is not unusual.

Land a loan. If you plan to apply for a bank or credit union loan, you will need a bulletproof business plan, a pristine credit record, and a top-drawer credit score (720 or higher). You might want to try a bank where you've been a longtime customer or one that is familiar with the franchise field. An

SBA-guaranteed bank loan can keep your down payment and monthly payments low. To find a bank offering one of these loans, check the SBA's website as well as the site's loans and grants search tool. Be sure to check to see if the franchise you're exploring has the SBA stamp of approval. SBA-approved franchises are ones whose disclosure agreements have been reviewed and accepted by the SBA. Applying for a preapproved franchise is easier and quicker.

To find the green-lighted list, go to the Franchise Registry (franchiseregistry.com). You can search by name if you have a certain franchise in mind or by industry. Plan on a down payment of 20 to 30 percent of the loan amount. Lenders will want you to have the proverbial skin in the game.

Seek expert advice. Don't go it alone. An accountant or lawyer with experience in franchising can help you gauge the entire franchise package and tax implications. For more information, go to the American Franchisee Association (franchisee.org), a national trade association of franchisees and dealers with over seven thousand members; the International Franchise Association (franchise.org) is a membership organization of franchisers, franchisees, and suppliers.

FRANCHISING TIPS
FROM THE SMALL BUSINESS ASSOCIATION

Here's how to start investigating a particular franchise that interests you:

* Request an information packet from the franchiser.

* Interview owners of current franchises.

* Research the industry and other franchises in this industry.

- Seek expert advice to better understand the franchise agreement.

- Review the costs related to getting into this franchise and compare them to the costs of starting a nonfranchised business in this industry.

Check out these links:

- The American Franchisee Association (AFA) (franchisee .org), a national trade association of franchisees and dealers with over seven thousand members.

- The American Association of Franchisees & Dealers (aafd .org), an organization that, among other things, has developed fair franchising standards for franchisers to adopt.

- The International Franchise Association (franchise.org), which offers franchise information.

- Unhappy Franchisee (unhappyfranchisee.com), which details franchises gone wrong.

- Blue MauMau (bluemaumau.org), a website with information and actual accounts of the ins and outs of franchising.

CHAPTER FOURTEEN

From the Corporate Ladder to the Pulpit

After graduating cum laude from the University of Chicago in 1971, Diane Rhodes landed a job with Illinois Bell Telephone Company and moved on to AT&T's New Jersey headquarters in 1979. She made a classic climb up the corporate ladder, juggling managerial duties with earning an MBA. For years, she traveled the country to conduct sales training and speak at industry conferences, addressing up to four hundred listeners at a pop.

When AT&T began trotting out early-retirement packages, Rhodes didn't qualify. In fact, she was busy developing programs to help with downsizing, including job counseling for employees. But she found herself thinking: What might I do if I had the chance?

And then the offer came. "I was proud to work for the corporation, but I had the feeling that maybe I was being called to something else, something more," recalls Rhodes, her blue eyes softening. So at age forty-nine, she snapped up an enticing early-retirement package and withdrew from AT&T's corporate cocoon, a world that had shaped her adult life.

Like many people who retire young, she was badgered by her contemporaries about what was next. She waited. She spent the next year dabbling in administrative jobs at her church. "You really have to take the time to be unsettled until the opportunity presents itself to you," she says. "It's hard to let ourselves live in that tension of the unknown, of not having the questions answered."

Ultimately, Rhodes was led by her faith. She enrolled in a course at Drew Theological School and began working as an executive assistant to the dean of the seminary. Five years later, she graduated summa cum laude with a master of divinity degree.

Eventually, Rhodes was ordained an Episcopal priest. "It was a breathless moment," Rhodes says. "Something metaphysically happens." Today, she is the rector at St. Andrew's Episcopal Church in Harrington, New Jersey.

But she knows in this line of work, moves to other churches are always possible. Regardless of where she is sent, her salary resides about a third of her former pay. Luckily, she doesn't fancy sporty cars, designer duds, or deluxe vacations. She prefers to read, do needlepoint, walk, and listen to classical music.

Rhodes is in charge of all the liturgical and spiritual life of the parish. It's a small parish—averaging fifty to sixty worshipers on a Sunday morning. She presides over baptisms, weddings, and funerals, as well as worship services. She regularly visits three nursing homes. "You make eye contact and look beyond into the heart and soul of a person who needs to know that he or she still matters and is a child of God," says Rhodes. She also delivers her sermons to her eighty-nine-year-old mother, who lives in an assisted-living community.

Before leaving AT&T, Rhodes had divorced. Her home was sold and the profits split. She put money down on a condo. Savings from her 401(k) plan plus her pension buyout provide her retirement fund. She has retiree healthcare coverage, to which she contributes.

The corporate-speaking gigs have given way to heartfelt sermons to her parishioners, amid the soaring beams and stained-glass windows of her tiny church. The audience may be smaller than in her AT&T days, she says, but the spiritual message is deeper.

The hours are still long, more than sixty a week, yet the rhythm is different. Rhodes once caught a train in New York's Penn Station, and a young woman with tears in her eyes saw her white collar and asked to talk. Rhodes paused in her journey to take the time to listen, giving new meaning to the idea of working overtime.

I asked Diane to look back and share her thoughts on her transition to the world of liturgy.

What did the career transition mean to you personally?

I knew. I had sensed for some time that I was being called in another direction. I did not know at first what it was I wanted to do. But as a person of faith, I have always believed that God issues invitations to us in a number of areas, and we have the freedom to either accept them or not.

I knew there was something going on, that I was being invited to move in a new direction in my life. I just didn't know quite what that was, so when the opportunity came to leave and retire with a package that included health benefits, I just decided it was time to take that risk and do some discernment, and to have the time to do the discernment.

And so I did and began to explore the possibilities of a call to the Episcopal priesthood. I took a few classes at the seminary, and I knew that is where I needed to be. I began the discussion process with my own parish priest and within our diocese. There are rules for that process. I formed a discernment committee who worked with me and prayed with me and was admitted to the ordination process at the Episcopal Church here in the diocese of Newark. I began the seminary part-time, graduated five years later, was ordained the next year to the diaconate, and finally to the priesthood.

Were you confident that you were doing the right thing? Any second-guessing?

I think we always second-guess and wonder, and yet, I guess I would say second-guessing isn't the word I would use. I would say there are always unanswered questions, and you have to be able to live within the uncertainty of not having things spelled out. The answers aren't there yet. I would call it a leap of faith; someone else might call it a leap of enthusiasm. It's a willingness to go and do something new and different. People experience that in different ways.

Anything you would have done differently?

Not really. I wish I had figured it out a little sooner, but changes like this require time. You can't make them in a hurry. You have to have the time.

How do you measure your success?

That is something I struggle with. It is not something you measure just in terms of how many people attend on Sunday, although that is something that you look at. Our little parish here is growing; I think you feel a growing level of trust and community with the people you serve as well as with the larger diocese. And that is a sign of success. I look at all the opportunities I have had to promote justice and equality within my community and in the larger community. Did I do that? How have I stepped up to this opportunity?

How big a role did financial rewards play in your decision to make a transition?

Most clergy don't go into it for the financial rewards. That is not why you choose this vocation. But the income is helpful. My mother lives in an assisted-living community. That's a real part of my financial reality. Her assets are gone, and so in a very loving way that is now my responsibility.

How did your preparation help you succeed?

I took the time to go back to school and pieced it together with partial scholarships. I worked and talked to people who were doing it. I had always been involved for many years as an active layperson in my parish. Out of those ministries came the beginnings, the first stirrings of the fact that I might be called to ordained ministry. Then knowing and working with many fine clergy within our diocese, the idea began to take shape and grow.

What do you tell people who ask for your advice?

I serve on our commission on ministry, and I work with people who believe they have a calling. For this vocation, we see it as a three-way call. It is what the person believes they may be called to do. It is also what the community and the church are saying. Is there validation of the call that an individual feels that they may be experiencing? What in their parish life supports that?

> "You really have to take the time to be unsettled until the opportunity presents itself to you. It's hard to let ourselves live in that tension of the unknown, of not having the questions answered."

That can take a great deal of time. We give people helpful questions to think about: How long have you been thinking about the ministry? What would happen if the church says no? Would you continue to be a faithful person? There are also the nuts and bolts things you need to contemplate if you want to make this kind of career move. Do you accept that there is not a large financial reward? Do you realize that if you are called to be a rector or pastor, you are going to be called to do things like fix the toilet if it breaks? All of the wonderful spiritual side of this life is countered by the realities—and there are chores to do.

What books or resources did you use or recommend others to use?

Aside from the Scriptures? That is a big piece of it. There are always those long dark nights when you think, have I done the right thing? Is it going to work? You need to find a way to center yourself and create some place of peace amid the uncertainty. For me, I found it between Robert Frost's poetry and the Forty-Sixth Psalm.

What are some of the surprises and unexpected rewards?

The absolute delight of working with individuals and congregations. I knew it would be wonderful, but when people invite you to share in the sacred moments of their lives—the happy ones or the ones that are hard, troubling, and sad—it is such a privilege to be invited into that sacred space. And it never fails to fill me with awe, and I am so grateful for that.

TEN TIPS TO GET YOU SPEAKING LIKE A PRO

Your future career may not include giving sermons; however, you could easily find yourself with an audience that you'll want to reach and connect with. Since 1924 Toastmasters International has helped many people from all walks of life increase their speaking skills and self-confidence in front of an audience. Toastmasters has nearly 292,000 members in 14,350 clubs in 122 countries. Most meetings consist of approximately twenty people who meet weekly for an hour or two. Participants practice and learn skills of effective speech: focus, organization, language, vocal variety, and body language.

Here are Toastmasters' top ten ways (and my take on them) to help rein in those stomach butterflies and give smooth, self-assured presentations:

1. *Know your material.* Be an expert. Know your material backwards and forwards. When you're speaking about

something you really know, it shines through to your audience. Importantly, it gives you the inner confidence to turn your talk into a conversation with friends. It opens the door for the material to come to life with personal anecdotes and a dollop of humor.

2. *Practice. Practice. Practice.* Repetition is the name of the game. It's important to practice your speech many times, so you're truly familiar with it. Pay attention to the pace of your talk. Slow down and breathe. Record your delivery, and pay close attention to those pesky "ums" and other filler words that sneak in inadvertently. Time your talk.

3. *Know the room.* Do a walk-through at the venue. Get there early, and check out the room where you'll be speaking. If you can get up on the stage or podium ahead of time, do it. Test check any equipment you may be using such as a PowerPoint presentation, where you will be using a clicker. This is not always possible, but it doesn't hurt to ask.

4. *Know the audience.* Paint a mental picture. Before you start your speech, do a quick mental exercise. Imagine yourself talking, your strong, vibrant voice flowing forth. Visualize your easy smile, and the audience nodding and clapping as you finish your talk.

5. *Relax.* Make some "new" friends ahead of time. If you're speaking to a group where you don't know anyone, make it your business to meet one or two people who will be part of your audience as folks are gathering. If you're there with time to spare, this kind of relaxed meet-and-greet ahead of time can take the edge off. And when you gaze out at a few familiar faces, even if they are new acquaintances, it's reassuring. You might even work in a

shout-out to one or two by name as you speak to illustrate a point. It gives your talk a conversational sense of familiarity to it.

6. *Visualize yourself giving your speech.* Step up to the microphone, take a deep breath, and smile. Do this before you utter one word. This can be very centering. Then ask your audience a question that's related to your topic that gets them involved straightaway. A show of hands is one way to do this. The physical movement alone energizes the room, and you, too. If you can work in a bit of humor at the top, it can break the ice. But don't try too hard. Not everyone can pull this off.

7. *Realize that people want you to succeed.* Remember no one wants you to fail. Keep in mind that your audience wants you to be a star. They want you to amuse, to teach, and to succeed.

8. *Don't apologize for any nervousness or problems.* Skip the mea culpa if you think your nervousness is showing. Chances are no one even detects it. Most people are so caught up in their own heads; they aren't paying that close attention to the nuances that only you can feel.

9. *Concentrate on the message—not the medium.* Stay present. Look outward, not inward. Make eye contact with audience members. Connect. Feel the energy. This will keep you from getting trapped by the nervous thoughts racing through your head. This is show time. Turn your charm on, and say to yourself. "Be the best that you can be today." Then when you look out at your audience and see their faces, meet their gaze. Feel the podium under your hands and the warm lights on your face, and focus your mind on the material you're sharing. You'll forget all about your fears.

10. *Gain experience.* Do it. The more you practice speaking, the easier it gets. Accept invitations to talk at local libraries, book clubs, and investment groups, anything really that gets you up and out in front of a group—even if it's ten people. The more experience you get, the more self-assured you will be. Bring a takeaway for your audience members to go home with—perhaps a handout that contains the highlights of your key advice, action steps, or web and other resources they can go to learn more about your topic. And don't forget your business card.

Go Where the Jobs Are

Some people leap into a second career they've always dreamed about, whether it's opening a boutique or joining a nonprofit group. Others, however, know they're ready for a change—but aren't sure what to change into. If you're seeking a more rewarding career and not necessarily one that involves your hobby or revolves around your steady interests, a good place to start is where jobs are available. Here are some of the top job-growth areas in which midcareer changers are likely to find work that's both meaningful and challenging.

Clergy. With widespread worries about the economy, war, and terrorism, it's not surprising that religion is a growth area these days—it's the underpinning of American culture, in many respects. Many clerics spend the bulk of their time ministering to parishioners in their homes. There are, of course, those inspirational sermons from the pulpit, and regular duties like officiating at baptisms and weddings and consoling people in times of grief.

Most clergy, despite the image, don't take a vow of poverty: The median expected salary for a typical pastor in the United States is $86,413, according to Salary.com. The median expected salary for a typical chaplain in the healthcare field in the United States is $52,155. Educational requirements vary according to denomination. Many require a graduate degree. Others will admit anyone who is called to the vocation. To learn more, speak to a clergyperson of your faith.

One particular niche that is on the rise is the job of hospice chaplain. Chaplains are a source of solace and support for patients with terminal illnesses and their families. It's heart-wrenching work, but the love you give is the love you get. Chaplains typically work as a team member with medical staff and outside clergy to offer spiritual sustenance and comfort to patients with seriously advanced illnesses. Covered under Medicare, Medicaid, and most private insurance plans, hospice care is a swiftly growing area in the healthcare field.

The chaplain's role in hospice care is so vital that the Centers for Medicare & Medicaid Services requires all hospice centers that receive reimbursements from the agency to employ a hospice chaplain, sometimes called a pastoral or spiritual counselor. About 1.65 million people received new or continuing hospice care last year, more than twice as many as did a decade ago, according to the National Hospice and Palliative Care Organization (NHPCO), an Alexandria, Virginia–based industry group. As demand for hospice care has increased, so have the number of programs nationwide. Today, there are about fifty-three hundred providers, up from about thirty-three hundred five years ago, according to NHPCO.

There is an array of employers in this field ranging from home health agencies, independent hospice facilities, nursing homes, and hospitals. Hours tend to be flexible and employees are expected to be available weekends and evenings.

This is a fairly unregulated field. Even under the government regulatory language that stipulates that a hospice that receives government funding have a spiritual counselor, it does not specify the qualifications of that position, other than the professional must be competent to function in that role. Hospice chaplains, therefore, can be ordained clergy or simply a hospice-trained individual who has experience in spiritual support. Many hospice providers will require a bachelor's degree in religious studies. Others require a master's degree in counseling, divinity, theology, social work, psychotherapy, psychology, or pastoral counseling.

For more information, contact the NHPCO or the Association of Professional Chaplains, which certifies healthcare chaplains. Check for job listings at local hospices or the big job boards such has Career Builder (careerbuilder.com) and Simply Hired (simplyhired.com).

Healthcare. The U.S. Department of Labor lists a variety of home and personal healthcare jobs as fast-growing occupations. An aging population and longer life expectancies as well as new treatments and technologies will boost employment growth for years to come in the health field.

In fact, for the period 2012 to 2022, according to the U.S. Bureau of Labor Statistics, the industry with the largest employment growth to come in terms of sheer numbers, by far, is healthcare and social assistance. It's projected to generate about one-third of all new jobs in the U.S. economy during the decade. Occupations and industries related to healthcare—which include public and private hospitals, nursing and residential care facilities, and individual and family services—are projected to add the most new jobs, 15.6 million, during the decade.

You don't have to be a surgeon or an intensive care unit nurse; there are hundreds of areas of specialization where you can attain a certification via a community college program or association to ramp up the necessary skills. Some of these include home health aide or personal care assistant, senior fitness trainer, audiologist, massage therapist, physical therapist, wellness coach, and home-modification pro (someone who is certified by the National Association of Homebuilders to retrofit homes for seniors and those with disabilities).

Many of these are jobs that ride the age wave and are on the rise to cater to the aging population. New ones are cropping up all the time. Health-related jobs, for example, might include music therapists for Alzheimer's patients and patient advocates to help people navigate the healthcare system. But they can also be jobs that use your current skills, such as technical chops for medical transcription services, finance, or project management know-how redeployed to the healthcare arena.

One person I know, for instance, took early retirement from his federal government desk job in his mid-fifties and turned his love for fixing things—a weekend hobby—into a job at a local hospital fixing wheelchairs, gurneys, and such. He loves the tinkering and the always-a-new-challenge aspect of the work, and he has flexible hours.

You'll find useful details about healthcare jobs in the U.S. Bureau of Labor Statistics' *Occupational Outlook Handbook* and the American Medical Association's *Health Care Careers Directory*. Another helpful website is Health Professions Network (healthpronet.org), which features different allied health professions.

Education. This is a popular second career for many people looking to find work with meaning and social impact. You can enroll at community colleges and in state-approved or private programs to transfer your professional skills to the classroom. Be forewarned: the jobs in the highest demand tend to be in special education, English as a second language, and math and science related. There's also a need for substitute teachers, tutors, and corporate trainers. Moreover, there are adult teaching opportunities at community colleges—often a good place to find work. You might also find openings in counseling and coaching at a range of organizations from the private sector to nonprofits to government agencies.

A good website for finding more about transitioning to education is Teach.org, an Education Department site that catalogs, by state, alternative certification programs and licensing and certification as well as state-specific teacher openings. Other sites to tap into are All Education Schools (alleducationschools.com), Teachers-Teachers .com, California Teacher Corps (cateachercorps.org), National Association for Alternative Certification (alt-teachercert.org), American Board for Certification of Teacher Excellence (abcte.org), and National Center for Education Information (ncei.com). These sites provide information about programs, teacher preparation, certification, and licensing.

Elder care. You might already be informally providing this type of help for your own parents—from shopping to cooking meals to offering personal care and companionship. If you're suited to it, there's plenty of need for paid workers at assisted-living homes, memory-care centers for Alzheimer's patients, and traditional nursing homes. Plus venues for elder care keep multiplying as specialties evolve.

The aging population is also driving up demand for nutritionists, physical therapists, speech and language specialists, and activity aides, who help design programs to encourage socialization and provide entertainment and relaxation.

Patience and a sense of humor are prerequisites, and the work can be repetitive and challenging—sometimes physically. A good place to

learn more is the Caregiver Action Network (CAN) (caregiveraction
.org), a leading family caregiver organization working to improve the
quality of life for the more than sixty-five million Americans who care
for loved ones with chronic conditions, disabilities, disease, or the frail-
ties of old age. CAN serves a broad spectrum of family caregivers, ranging from the parents of children with special needs to the families and
friends of wounded soldiers, and from a young couple dealing with a
diagnosis of MS to adult children caring for parents with Alzheimer's
disease.

Pay varies widely, starting in the midtwenties and going much
higher. A personal and homecare aide might expect pay to be generally
$7.36 per hour to $12.45, but $35 or more per hour is possible, depend-
ing on experience and certification. There tends to be a lot of turnover,
so job openings are plentiful, especially helping the elderly in-home, as
well as at assisted living and hospice facilities. The median expected
salary for a typical home care dietitian in the United States is $59,479,
according to Salary.com.

Nonprofits. I've spent a fair amount of time discussing nonprofit
jobs so far, but my motivation is twofold. First, many career switchers
are eyeing work with meaning that makes a difference in the world at
this stage in life. And the good news is nonprofits fill that bill and are
hiring. In 2013, 44 percent of nonprofit groups said they planned to
hire more workers, up from only 33 percent two years ago, according to
a survey of more than 580 organizations by Nonprofit HR Solutions, a
human resources consulting firm.

Health nonprofits, followed by environment and animal-welfare
groups, were most likely to report plans to hire, according to the report.
From community outreach to finance to fundraising to program man-

agement to marketing and public relations, there's a range of skills that are in need.

But with all of these jobs, the essential prerequisite is a genuine passion for the nonprofit's mission. "Your commitment for the organization's cause is what will set you apart from other candidates," Laura Gassner Otting, president and CEO of Nonprofit Professionals Advisory Group, an executive search firm based in Boston, told me.

Depending on the size of the charity, the jobs may offer flexible hours and can be on a full- or part-time basis. Pay ranges vary based on factors such as the size of the nonprofit, experience, and where you live.

To hone your skills, you might consider taking workshop classes or enrolling in a certification program offered by the Association of Fundraising Professionals and the Foundation Center. The Foundation Center offers affordable classes nationwide in classrooms and online that cover grant proposal writing and fundraising skills. Many colleges, universities, and community colleges also offer courses and certification programs in fundraising. The Public Relations Society of America and the American Marketing Association offer workshops and webinars on a variety of subjects you need to know now, such as social media and branding.

If you have a background as a chief financial officer, comptroller, or accountant, step on up to a financial post. A degree in accounting or business is generally required. The most common certification is a Certified Public Accountant (CPA). Encore.org has links to nonprofit job boards and videos and articles about nonprofit job hunting.

Job Sites

- AARP.org
- Careerbuilder.com
- Encore.org
- Retiredbrains.com
- Retirementjobs.com
- Seniors4hire.org
- Workforce50.com
- Workreimagined.aarp.org

Job sites specifically geared toward nonprofit work:

- Idealist.org
- Bridgespan.org
- Cgcareers.org
- Nonprofitprofessionals.com
- Foundationcenter.org
- Thenonprofittimes.com
- Philanthropy.com

CHAPTER FIFTEEN

Working It

Inside the basement of the McBurney Y in the Chelsea neighborhood of Manhattan, the Swedish group ABBA's 1970s hit "Dancing Queen" is blasting: "See that girl, watch that scene, diggin' the dancing queen."

Moving right along in rhythm is a line-up of thirty perspiring women and men, ranging in ages from sixty to eighty-five. There are no spring chickens here.

They're standing in jagged rows strewn across the wooden floor, clad in sneakers, T-shirts, leggings, and sweatpants, staring straight into a the big mirror reflecting their shaking images back at them.

Some of them can't resist smiling, as they raise a three-pound weight above their shoulders and down again, moving and grooving.

This Active Older Adults Power class is filled to capacity. The high-energy fifty-nine-year old instructor Roseann Brown is not surprised.

She has seen attendance double in these kinds of active adult exercise classes since she became a senior fitness instructor four years ago. Little wonder that the number of fitness clubs and gyms across the country offering these special classes is rapidly multiplying.

Brown has tapped into a growing field. As the population ages, jobs like senior fitness trainer and others in health-related arenas that serve their needs are on the rise.

And they don't require you to head back for an intensive and expensive course of study. Five years ago, when Brown decided to try her new path, she did her homework to see which certificate programs might fill the bill.

Employers and clients are increasingly accepting professional certifications as the cachet and proof of your expertise.

Brown's repertoire, for example, ranges from certifications in aqua aerobics and chair aerobics, where chairs are used for seated or standing support, to SilverSneaker classes to workouts that strengthen the body using techniques that emphasize balance, abdominal strength, and muscle control using techniques from yoga and dance. She has also studied low-intensity workouts designed for older adults with arthritis or other joint challenges, using light weights and Dyna-Bands, which are nationally certified by the Arthritis Foundation.

To teach these classes, Brown kicked off by earning a certificate via a written and performance exam with the Aerobics and Fitness Association of America (AFAA) to teach as group fitness instructor. Then tagged on the other qualifications. And she's currently studying for the AFFA-accredited Personal Trainer Certification, so she can work directly with a client without going through a fitness club or Y as the gatekeeper. Total out-of-pocket education cost to date: less than $1,000.

It's a dream job for Brown, who spent thirty-five years working in the garment industry selling teenage clothing wholesale. "The wholesale fashion business was shrinking," she recalled. "It was survival of the fittest as manufacturing went overseas. I saw the change coming. And knew I was going to have to do something new."

Moreover the work was stressful. "I wasn't going to get rich. I was helping my boss put extensions on his house," she said with a laugh.

Brown had a savings cushion set aside that allowed her the time to make her transition and prepared to learn to live on less, but love her work more—a fair trade-off in her mind.

She thought about how she could specialize in order to get a job and make money. "I planted myself in gyms, watched different classes and was struck by the number of older exercisers."

And she saw the opening. "As a senior fitness instructor, I was age appropriate. The basic fitness instructors are twenty-year-old kids. So I asked myself, how can I stand out? How can I be different? I've always gotten along well with seniors. I enjoy their company. Their stories are so fascinating. No divas need apply."

Then she asked instructors what training and certifications they had under their belt, and took action. Bingo, she had found her next act.

She leads seventeen classes a week to groups ranging in size from fifteen to forty seniors at a variety of locations and earns $40 to $50 an hour.

What's in it for her? "I have always loved to exercise, and I love being able to set my schedule. It doesn't feel like work. I need to move. I can't sit on a couch."

She now works four hours in the morning. Takes her afternoons off, and gets back to the paid workouts in the evening hours. "I work seven days a week. I would never have done that before, but I have a choice. I love it."

For these senior swingers, the motivation to work up a sweat a few times a week is generally because they want to be social, to stay fit and healthy, Brown says. "For some, their doctors told them they better do something and others are just looking to meet people their age."

Brown's aha moment: "I discovered I missed my calling. I should have been a gym teacher."

When she sees an arthritic client who once was unsteady on her feet and walking with a cane gradually grow steadier and more confident, it's a special reward. "It's magic," Brown says.

"When people say, 'Roseann, I could never do this before,' it just feels good. I'm adding to the quality of their lives, and it feels right."

Plus she's made new friends. "I even go to some of their homes for dinner sometimes and help them with their computers."

"I have always been a leader, never a follower, very independent. I was divorced at twenty-five and have been on my own ever since." Her mantra: "Exercise makes you stronger. It empowers you. That's a gift I can give back to these seniors."

I asked Roseann to look back and share her thoughts on her transition to a career as a senior fitness instructor.

What did the transition mean to you personally?

Freedom from the corporate world. Self-employment. It has allowed me to follow my passion, which is fitness.

Were you confident that you were doing the right thing? Any second-guessing?

I was confident from day one that I made the right choice. And I was grateful that I saved enough money from a job of thirty-five years in fashion, which allowed some financial security to be able to support myself until my new career took off.

Anything you would have done differently?

I'm a firm believer that everything in life happens when it is supposed to. But if I could go back in time, I would have made this career change sooner.

How do you measure your success?

That's a complicated question. I have several measures of success.... When a member of the gym returns day after day to my class. An applause after the class ends.... Smiling faces.... When I see one of my students getting stronger and more confident with the exercise.

How big a role did financial rewards play in your decision to make a transition?

Actually the opposite. I made a career change not for the money. I was paid extremely well in my past career. The career change was not about money. . . . It was about feeling fulfilled and happy to go to work every day.

How did your preparation help you succeed?

I prepared for two years before making a career change. I took several actions. I went to exercise workshops, watched many DVDs on the variety of exercises, and asked a lot of questions to other instructors.

What do you tell people who ask for your advice?

Don't quit your job unless you are certain of what's next for you.

And then . . . *just do it.*

What are some of the surprises and unexpected rewards?

The biggest surprise is that I work every day . . . weekends, too. . . . For now, it works for me, but eventually, I will change my work schedule. Rewards are the new friends I've made with my students.

Senior Fitness Instructor

Roseann Brown shared that she has always loved to exercise. If you know you're ready for a next act but are stuck on what that could be, you can try jotting down the things that come easily to you—the things you have loved to do since childhood. It can take some sleuthing. But you will be pleasantly surprised to find that once you take the time to do that, you will find your way to bundle those innate talents and craft work from it. And once you do, you're going to be the happiest you've been in a long time. With any luck, you will probably receive the financial payback you deserve because you are doing work based on your solid skills and talents.

Still stuck? Interview a few people you respect—friends, family, or colleagues—and ask them what they think you excel at. Believe me, most of us take our unique skills for granted. Pay attention to their responses. No doubt, you will see a pattern. That's a blueprint to start finding your path to a new career.

CHAPTER SIXTEEN

From Capitol Hill to Capitol Humor

It's Saturday night at the Fireplace Room, a classic cabaret setting in Washington, DC's Westin Hotel, and the place is packed with an eager audience of nearly one hundred. They're here to listen and laugh as performer Ken Rynne and pianist and singer Sean Collins take them on a rollicking ride through the latest social issues and political shenanigans in a lively evening of parodies, satire, and song.

The act, performing under the troupe's moniker, Planet Washington, has steadily been drawing in crowds to its au courant show since 2006, and little wonder. It's deliciously fun.

For one-time lawyer, congressional aide, and lobbyist Ken Rynne, "this is living the dream." And though it's little more than a mile from the hallowed halls of Congress—it's an entirely different venue.

Rynne's got the music in him, but it took him twenty-five years to turn it into a career. For the former choirboy, performing has been the thread that has run throughout his entire life. He sang with the Boston Symphony as a fourth grader and around the family television set during Mitch Miller sing-alongs in the sixties.

After graduating from the Boston Latin School, he was awarded a scholarship to go to the prestigious Eastman School of Music but turned it down. "I didn't think music was a serious career," Rynne says. "My dad was a Boston cop, and for some reason, I decided I should be a lawyer."

Rynne studied government at Georgetown University where he sang with the Chimes, Georgetown's a cappella group. During a college internship in the office of Speaker of the House Tip O'Neill, he contracted Potomac fever. "It was just fun. Politics and government was the thing," Rynne recalls. After graduation, he continued on to Georgetown Law School and then accepted a position practicing energy regulatory law at a DC firm.

But seven years later, the practice splintered, and Rynne headed to Capitol Hill to work for Senator Howard Metzenbaum on energy issues. Over the course of seven years he was Representative Joe Kennedy's legislative director and held staff positions with Senate Majority Leaders George Mitchell, Tom Daschle, and John Kerry. "Every day I felt jazzed, walking through those marble halls," Rynne recalls.

But his toes kept tapping. He wrote and performed in a dozen Hexagon shows—a nonprofit organization that produces an annual musical political satire show performed at the Duke Ellington School of the Arts in Washington. Rynne also moonlighted with the well-regarded Washington-based troupe the Capitol Steps.

With two young daughters and college tuitions to fund, the time had come to leave the Hill to make some real money. Rynne, like many ex-Hill insiders, signed on as a lobbyist. He started with the

American Institute of Architects, which was followed by a stretch with credit card giant MBNA America in Delaware.

His annual salary ballooned from $35,000 as a Hill staffer to a healthy six figures as a lobbyist. He reveled in the newfound dough, shelling out for a flashy Jaguar to tool around in, and buying a Mc-Mansion in the suburbs.

But he was lost outside the Capitol Beltway. He found himself drawing up business plans for his own fantasy Washington revue during business meetings, writing musical comedy sketches, and yearning for the spotlight and the laughter. He daydreamed of starting his own show around the theme Washington, DC: The Musical.

In late 2004, his boss and mentor at MBNA retired, and Rynne knew he needed to break free of the so-called golden handcuffs. "I had been a bit out of place there from the beginning," he says. "I was the proverbial round peg in the square hole. I missed the excitement of Washington politics but wasn't clear on exactly what I should be doing."

The next year, he said farewell to MBNA. Through the firm's human resources department, he learned about Right Management, a consulting firm that specializes in helping executives like Rynne evaluate career options and develop a personal action plan. Through a series of diagnostic tests, they pinpointed two areas that would suit him: education and entertainment.

Bingo. The light went on, Rynne remembers. "That came out as a nice affirmation of where my heart had always been. I decided to move back to DC and try the comedy stuff but put a time limit on it." If it did not take off in five years, he would go do what his younger daughter called "a real job."

Newly single and his daughters now adults, he was free to strike out on a newfangled path. "I'm in the business of following my heart now," Rynne says.

He sold the big house and car in favor of a rented apartment in Georgetown. And he began to piece together his new enterprise, modeled in part after the Capitol Steps. He set up an LLC corporation called Planet Washington; created a website (planetwashington .com); and linked up with mentor Mark Russell, the master of political satire; and found a collaborator to man the keyboards.

The heart of the show was there. "The writing is easy. It just comes to me. That's the core. Singing, I have been doing forever. That's part of me. That's easy. It's marketing. I had a very naive view of marketing and the nuts and bolts of running the business side."

So Rynne signed up for a community college course to learn how to market a small business. He participated in comedy workshops to hone his material. He reached out to other performers in the city for strategies. And he networked like mad to raise investment capital to get the show on the road and pay for everything from equipment to advertising.

By November 2006, Rynne was ready to hit the stage. He did his first show for an audience of seventy paying patrons. He had the show videotaped to use as a marketing tool when he met with bookers and hotel and restaurant managers to drum up interest. Gradually, he landed a handful of rooms to play, starting with the National Press Club, a natural for his politically savvy act.

But he was naive about show business for a struggling new comedy act. "I had no idea how long it would take to get a cabaret booking. Someone will come in one night, catch the act, and say they want to book us—they're serious, but it can be months before that actually happens," he says. "I thought they would all come running."

Money has been tight. Gigs have come slower than Rynne had expected, but he has hung in there, stretching to meet his monthly budget. Now with steady shows each month, he can easily cover his rent and expenses. But he protects himself financially by taking on contract lawyering assignments that he taps using his legal background, mostly reviewing documents in litigation. Plus he hired a marketing assistant to help him pitch his act to the college and association markets, which is starting to pay off with speaking and performances on campuses around the country.

And he's confident the big break is coming. "Business keeps growing," says Rynne with a wide smile. "I'm happy. I'm living the life. Who needs a Jag when you can have laughter?"

I asked Ken to look back and share his thoughts on his transition to a career in comedy.

What did the transition mean to you personally?

I wasn't very happy working at the bank but was caught up in making the money. Soon I had trouble even going to work. It was hard work to get there. Let me put it this way: They gave me an alarm clock as a gag gift when I left MBNA.

Now the hardest work is filling the room with people. I love writing and performing on stage. I'm in the zone when I'm on stage. People react to me. Everyone gets it. I love it. I write at night, writing at two in the morning. I am working all the time, but it doesn't feel like work.

Were you confident that you were doing the right thing? Any second-guessing?

> I feel certain about my decision today coming off a successful show this weekend. But not always. About a month ago, when I was looking at my financial situation I started wondering. I have some doubts, but they are purely financial. At this point, I'm in it. I don't want to ask, What if? I want to push this thing as far as it goes.

Anything you would have done differently?

> From a technical angle, I incorporated as an LLC. I thought it was important to have a business entity for all this money that was coming in. It was expensive to do, and there are a lot of reporting requirements. There was probably an easier way to do it.

> I wouldn't have been so naive. I'm not a businessperson. I'm creative. I should have managed my money better to have more saved for the start-up period. But I think I am pretty much where I am supposed to be. I only wish I had done it sooner!

How do you measure your success?

> My metrics are laughter and applause. Laugher is tough to get. I know I'm fine if I'm paying the bills. It will be great to be in a position where I have to choose between gigs. "Sorry. I am doing the president's dinner that night . . . can't be in Boston."

How big a role did financial rewards play in your decision to make a transition?

I'm not independently wealthy, so I need money to pay the bills. But I am not expecting to get a Jaguar again.

> "I'm happy. I'm living the life. Who needs a Jag when you can have laughter?"

How did your preparation help you succeed?

I probably should have done more. It started as a daydream, and I thought about it for a long time, fantasized about it, visualized it, and wrote a plan. But then I had to get off the stool and start doing it, and that was harder than I thought it would be. Keeping a day job while I got rolling would have provided less financial stress.

What are some of the surprises and unexpected rewards?

Having my mentor political satirist Mark Russell laugh at my stuff. He recently sent me a note and referred to me as "a colleague." I graduated from being an apprentice to being a colleague. That's validation—something we comedians always need.

What books or resources did you use or recommend other to use?

The personality and career diagnostic tests from Right Management helped me focus, and know I was heading in the right direction.

What advice do you give to people who ask you for your advice?

I ask them a few simple questions: What do you want to do? What would you rather be doing? Know anybody making money at that? What do they say?

To thine own self be true. Do what you love and the money will follow. I have that saying framed and hanging on my office wall.

KEY THINGS TO CONTEMPLATE BEFORE MAKING A MAJOR CAREER CHANGE

Marketing 101. How good are you at selling yourself? Really? This is a key ingredient for those of you embarking on an entrepreneurial second act. This is a genuine blind spot that wannabe second actors can possess.

You may have had a wonderful initial experience starting a new business or a consulting business but fail to understand that your confidence is only part of the battle; the other part is marketing yourself as you move along from those heady first few months or even years. For people who have worked in a setting where they did their job and delivered the end result to much fanfare, this change can be extremely difficult.

Greenhorn blues. It's much tougher than you think to cope with being a beginner. It's unnerving. You feel as though the rug had been pulled out from under you, and your base of support and confidence slipped away. To have a second-act hit, you must be sufficiently open to change in life. Career changers often underestimate what the transition will bring and how many things they actually appreciate in their lives. All of a sudden, they realize how they miss their old career or the trappings of it, and they are not really open to replacing those things.

Respect. We all like to be treated with respect. We enjoy the admiration, esteem, and appreciation we get from colleagues, people we manage at our current jobs, our bosses, and others whom we come into contact with both socially and professionally. We take pleasure when those around us have a high opinion of us.

But when you move into uncharted territory, you're a neophyte, the proverbial new kid on the block, starting over at the bottom. This requires some psychological adjustment and fine-tuning. All of a sudden, you are making less, probably making a few mistakes, and not being treated like the experienced professional you have come to be.

Look inside and recognize those feelings. You might even want to hire a professional such as a therapist or career coach to guide you through this more personal adjustment. A supportive partner or best friend might be all the shoring up you need, but it is a transition phase that shouldn't be ignored.

Making mistakes gracefully. Easier said than done. Face it, the older you are and further along on your professional success ladder, the harder it is to accept criticism and responsibility for screwing up. Your ego just isn't as nimble and forgiving as it once was. This is the reality, and it happens when you start anew. When you're in your twenties you are better equipped to handle the inevitable screw-ups and missteps, let them slide off your back with a simple shrug, and move on.

When you can accept that trying new things means learning from your mistakes along the way, you will be in a healthier, stronger place to move ahead. Doing things badly is just another step toward doing them well.

SPEAKING LIKE A PRO

Even if you aren't seeking the klieg lights like Ken Rynne does, you may find yourself front and center speaking to groups of people in an expert capacity. Here's key professional speaking advice from my mentoring session with professional speaker John Spence:

- *Don't do anything for free.* At the very least, get every client to make a small contribution in your name to your favorite local charity. It's a nice way to make sure that they will take your speech seriously—and donate money to a charity you care about.

- *Word-of-mouth referrals are the single greatest source of new speeches.* Get in the habit of asking your customers to please send a personal note with a strong referral to anyone they feel would benefit from hearing the speech you just delivered for them.

- *Check out the competition.* The best way to determine your price range is to look at five or six other speakers who are talking about a similar topic, and are on just about the same level as you, and then simply figure out a price that is about 85 percent of the average.

CHAPTER SEVENTEEN

For the Love of a Dog

Ten years ago, Linda Waitkus was weary after two decades in the retail business. She quit her job as store manager for Lord & Taylor in Philadelphia, got a golden retriever puppy she named Soleil, and took a course at a local women's club called "What Do You Want to Do?"

The course was enlightening in its simplicity. The instructor asked: What do you do when you're off of work? What do you like? What magazines do you read?

Waitkus focused. She loved interior design and her dog, who went everywhere with her. But a year or so later, after trying out a few other ventures, she was still not sure what she wanted to do with the rest of her life.

Her ex-boss came calling and offered her another executive job, and she was back in the retail frenzy once again, managing a flagship Bloomingdale's, outside of Washington, DC.

In a blink of an eye, Waitkus had clocked three decades in the retail business. And the old feelings of burnout were back. The urge to retire hit hard, but this time she had saved enough in her employer's 401(k) retirement plan and other accounts to do it.

During her second retail stint, her love of dogs had grown even deeper. She spent all her free time with Soleil, going for long walks, taking her to dog shows to compete and learning how to groom golden retrievers for the show ring.

When she heard through her community grapevine about a local pet retail shop owner eager to sell her shop, something clicked. She knew what she wanted to do.

She didn't need to get out of retail, after all. "I am so good at it ... always been successful, so I just transferred to a different commodity and a different stage where I can work for myself," Waitkus says.

It was the message she remembered from her course ten years back. "Take what you are great at and make it what you want it to be," she recalls.

Waitkus began to map a strategy to buy the store. She carefully spent a year developing a solid business plan. She sought guidance from other pet shop owners and suppliers to learn how the business runs. Better yet, she was fortunate to have enough funds saved outside of her retirement accounts to finance her new venture.

So four years ago, she officially retired from Bloomingdale's and bought the eighteen-hundred-square-foot pet store. Now she sells everything a dog or cat lover would want from healthful food to toys and accessories, plus offers grooming services.

This is her working retirement. "I'm a saver and have enough money set aside for the day I'm truly retired to live comfortably. All I need out of my business now is living expenses," she says.

At fifty-eight, she has no regrets about taking an early retirement and starting over as an entrepreneur. "I ran a $75-million department store but had to learn how to sell a bag of dog food," she says with a laugh. "I was successful in my retail career because I'm a very hands-on person, so I was always on the floor walking with people, selling, too. I wasn't afraid to fold shirts or clean up fitting rooms. My biggest claim to fame as a general manager was being a part of it."

And that's precisely what she still does, dropping to her knees to pet or hand a treat to every four-legged customer that trots through the door. She remembers all their names.

Since its first year of business, her shop, Great Dogs of Great Falls, has turned a profit, and she's been able to pay herself a salary. Today, she employs two full-time groomers and two bathers, plus an assistant manager to help run the six-day-a-week operation. "I did retire, but I planned carefully, and the gift I gave to myself is freedom of doing what I love—playing with dogs," Waitkus says.

I asked Linda to look back and share her thoughts on her transition to being a small business owner.

What did the transition mean to you personally?

It meant owning my own future by having my own business. I enjoy the thought of working for myself. My dogs, who are my family, get to be with me twenty-four hours a day, which is huge for me. I didn't have to worry about them being home by themselves. It was also a really good ego booster, too, because I was able to have a goal and accomplish it.

Were you confident that you were doing the right thing? Any second-guessing?

No. No. No. No second-guessing. I was really confident on this one.

Anything you would have done differently?

Nope.

How do you measure your success?

Number one is the loyalty of my clients. The fact that they are my constant buddies coming in and out is really special. Some of them I have bonded with as friends. It is exactly what I wanted—a neighborhood store. The people coming in and out are my neighbors. I know every single person who walks in.

Business-wise, I admit, I wasn't sure I was making the greatest decision because it was in a small traffic area. But I don't think I would be as happy if it was in an area that was just in and out, in and out, in and out and impersonal business.

How big a role did financial rewards play in your decision to make a transition?

Not much at all. All I wanted was a living. I have been able to maintain a good lifestyle. I am not making a fortune by any means, but I am maintaining a lifestyle.

How did your preparation help you succeed?

Definitely my savings helped me be prepared. The other thing is I had so much background in what I was going into. I knew retail so well after thirty years of experience. I knew what I was doing. And I was and am to this day very clear on the image I wanted to put out. I don't deviate from my image.

The image is upscale without being stuffy. It is comfortable, high-end merchandise but not chi chi. Great Falls is a wealthy community, but also a down-to-earth one. From the colors I picked in the store to the products I carry to how I display it, are all reflective of this very rural area, close to DC. It's all about the love the land.

What do you tell people who ask for your advice?

Prepare. People come in and say, "I want a store like this. It looks so easy." It is not easy. I have the background and knowledge of how to do it from thirty years of a career. So do something you know you are good at, and that you love. Don't do it so haphazardly that you won't be successful. I had a complete business plan that I spent a year or so formulating. I read a lot of books.

I took my time developing the tagline for the store: "Caring for our neighborhood dogs inside and out." I lived that. It took me a long time to come up with that sentence, but it means a lot to me because it's what the store mission is. Every time I do anything that is what I follow.

Get a mentor. I had a mentor who introduced me to a vendor. And that vendor turned me on to stores he thought were great. I spent months driving as far as a hundred-mile radius even, looking at all the dog stores out there.

What are some of the surprises and unexpected rewards?

Rewards are all the acquaintances and friends I've made. The surprise is the amount of effort. I thought because I had worked the big stores and was a somewhat workaholicy personality that this would be a cakewalk.

But there is all the little stuff, paying the bills and buying paper towels. These are the things as a small businessperson that you must realize. You are responsible for everything. There are no days off. I still get to do grooming two days a week, then selling two days a week and one day of running the store. And while I do I try to take two days off, they get incorporated with doing business things.

When you own a business, everything you do has a little part of it in it. When I go to Costco, say, I meet people, and I say, "Oh yeah, I have a pet store and here's my card." It's networking!

DOLLARS AND CENTS ADVICE
FOR STARTING A BUSINESS

I say it all the time, debt is a dream killer. But here's the good news. If you're in decent financial shape with no debt, or very little, beyond a mortgage, perhaps, you have myriad options for funding your startup. Here are the basics:

Don't wager your retirement funds. Do not put your whole 401(k), or even half, into this great idea. It is possible to borrow from your 401(k), or use the money you have stashed away in a Roth IRA, but be cautious here. With people living longer, healthier lives, you want to save as much as you can in a tax-deferred plan to ensure that you don't outlive your money.

That's precisely what you have these savings to cushion, so tread lightly. Moreover, you could be subject to withdrawal penalties and income taxes, plus lose the tax-deferred compounding that could serve you well in retirement, if you don't pay the funds back in the required timeframe.

Take heart, though, there are plenty of other places to tap for the capital needed to get up and rolling. Here are some means to your end:

Personal savings. The truth is most startups, like Linda Waitkus's pet shop, are funded with personal savings. Before you make a big withdrawal I recommend that you have at least a year's worth of fixed living expenses, like your mortgage and insurance needs, set aside. When you're starting your own shop, you may have to forgo a salary for a few months, even a year, until you gain traction and income starts flowing.

Friends and family. Be clear about the terms and put everything in writing, so no bad blood arises. When career-changer Bill Skees, a former IT pro, needed funding to open his independent bookstore Well Read New & Used Books, in Hawthorne, New Jersey, he asked his six siblings for a handout. The rate on his family loans: 3.5 percent. "At the time I was starting up in 2010, small-business bank loans were hard to get," says Skees. He raised $124,000 from them, borrowing on a three-year term. He and his wife, Mary Ann, tapped savings for the remaining startup costs of $78,000.

Banks and credit unions. Banks are not always easy to crack when it comes to small business lending. It goes without saying that you'll need a firm business plan and a squeaky clean credit record. Your first stop should be a bank that's familiar with you or your industry, or one that's known for having a soft spot for small-business lending. It's a good idea to seek out one that offers SBA-guaranteed loans—check the "Local Resources" page on the agency's website (sba.gov). SBA-guaranteed bank loans tend to demand a lower down payment and monthly payments may be more manageable. That said, a lender will probably want you to show that you have some skin in the game, too. That means you must be able to show that you have some capital or equity that you're prepared to personally invest into the business. A good resource to learn more is BusinessUSA (business.usa.gov), the federal government's site for entrepreneurs seeking small business loans. You can search by state to see what special programs might be available for you.

Angel investors and venture capital firms. This can be a high-wire dance, but if you can do a little soft-shoe and have a great idea and terrific business plan, these types of investors will back you in exchange for equity or partial ownership. If this route interests you, check out the SBA's Small Business Investment Company Program.

Economic development programs. There are a range of development loan programs out there, but it can take a little sleuthing, and you may need special certification. For example, if you're a woman, you might consider getting your firm certified as a woman-owned business. If you're the principal owner and from a minority group or are located in an economically disadvantaged region, you might qualify for a special loan as well. The SBA's economic development department resources can help you decide if this might be an avenue for you. If you're a veteran, the Department of Veterans Affairs, for instance, can provide you with information on how to get certified.

Corporate programs. Some big businesses offer small business start-up support as well. For instance, Michelin North America, based in Greenville, South Carolina, has provided low-interest financing—loans range from $10,000 to $100,000—to certain minority-owned and disadvantaged businesses, including women-owned firms, in parts of South Carolina.

Grants. Go to Grants.gov for information on more than a thousand federal grant programs. Female entrepreneurs may want to tap into one of the SBA's Women's Business Centers around the country. These centers provide state, local, and private grant information to women interested in going into business for themselves with either a nonprofit or for-profit organization.

Equity crowd-funding sites. These virtual fundraising campaigns generally raise small sums, but you never know, it can add up. A few years ago, Kickstarter (kickstarter.com), one such site, brought in more than $10 million for a fledgling watch company. It's easy to set up. You simply post a sketch of what your project is with a video, a target dollar amount, and a deadline. You blast out an email to friends, family, and colleagues and politely ask them to share your project and funding invitation with their friends, and so on.

When someone opts to donate to your cause, payments are made via a charge to their credit card via Amazon. Donors can pony up anywhere from $1 to thousands. It's not considered an investment. When you reach your goal, Kickstarter takes 5 percent, and you pay 3 to 5 percent to Amazon's credit card service. If you don't raise the money by the deadline, the pledges are canceled. Your contributors aren't charged for their donation, and Kickstarter takes nothing.

Other sites for raising seed money online include RockThe Post (rockthepost.com), a free network that helps entrepreneurs meet professionals and investors who can help via funds, time, or materials; Indiegogo (indiegogo.com); and AngelList (angel.co), which can connect you with angel investors. Because these are all fairly new, be sure to do your own background check on these sites.

Home equity loans. If you have substantial equity built up in your house and a credit score well above seven hundred, this route may be a pretty good option. The funds are usually taken as a lump sum that you can pay off over time. And interest is not sky high, under 5 percent right now.

Credit cards. Using plastic is certainly easy, but it's a risky choice. Most cards have double-digit interest rates on balances that roll over month to month. That's a pretty high bar to saddle a new company with in its early days. If you do want to go this route, check out Bankrate (bankrate.com) or Credit.com for a list of cards with the lowest rates and best terms right now.

CHAPTER EIGHTEEN

Three-Part Fitness Program

Part I: Getting Financially Fit

Debt is a dream killer. OK, there it is again. But it's true. Whatever your motivation for your second act, you still need to be pragmatic. For most people, a midcareer restart comes with a financial price tag, particularly if you don't have the cushion of a partner's income or a retirement or severance package. It might mean a sizable pay cut to pursue work in a more altruistic field, a hefty tuition bill for more schooling, or a temporary loss of medical and retirement benefits. If you're starting your own business, you will have start-up costs and may forego a salary for a year or so while the business gains traction.

If you're in good financial shape, you can be nimble. It opens up choices when it comes to starting a new career, embarking on your own business, paying the tuition to go back to school to gain skills, and much more.

But before you plunge into a second career, it pays to make a financial plan that will allow you to stick with your goals. If you're likely to trade a good income for better work, first review your entire financial life, from everyday expenses to retirement funding and health insurance costs. Then consider some of these money moves to set yourself up for success:

1. Chart a budget. You might need to live on less, at least initially, when you start over in a new field or ramp up a small business venture. A snapshot of your income, debts, and savings will help you see where you can make some adjustments. Ask what luxuries you can do without: Restaurants? Dry-cleaning? Vacations? Two cars?

2. Sock away an emergency fund. A savings cushion of roughly a year of living expenses to pay for transition costs, as well as unexpected emergencies, will keep you from dipping into home equity or retirement savings—and paying penalties—later.

My advice is to stay liquid. Emergency funds typically belong in bank accounts or money market funds that don't fluctuate in value and are easily accessible by check, ATM, or teller window (I also suggest putting some of your emergency cash in bank CDs with maturity dates of six months or less so you can eke out a little more interest (they currently yield up to 1 percent).

Generally speaking, you'll probably find the highest rates at online banks and credit unions. A great place to comparison shop is Bankrate (bankrate.com).

I keep my emergency stash in a federally insured money-market account where I can make withdrawals at any time without penalty.

It's now paying 0.84 percent, which is actually terrific considering these accounts now offer 0.05 percent to 0.86 percent nationwide, according to Bankrate. Interest-bearing checking accounts have similar yields, according to DepositAccounts.com.

Before socking away money in a bank account billing itself as high-yield, check to see if there are any restrictions. There may be fees for withdrawing money more than a set number of times each month or a monthly balance requirement. I also keep some cash at home.

3. Get your credit report. Many employers review it. So do lenders, insurers, and landlords. Check for mistakes by obtaining a free annual report at AnnualCreditReport.com. Fix any errors.

4. Boost your credit score. Best moves to improve: Always pay your bills on time. One late payment packs a wallop. Don't open new accounts, transfer balances, or close accounts if you know a lender might pull it anytime soon.

5. Pay down debt. This can take some time, but starting a new venture with as clean a balance sheet as you can will make a difference, particularly in the lean days of your new venture when you need to be financially fit.

6. Downsize. Depending on the real estate market where you live, you might refinance your mortgage or sell your home and downsize to a smaller home or move to town where the cost of living is lower.

7. Shop for health insurance. If you're switching to self-employment or going to work for a small business or nonprofit that does not offer a health insurance plan, shop for insurance on the new health-care exchanges via Healthcare.gov. Don't drop your current job insurance (you can continue it for a time under a law known as COBRA) until you have a new policy in place. Note that with COBRA, you will likely lose your employer's contribution so be prepared.

Open a health savings account. This smart, tax-advantaged

financial tool, which works in combination with a health insurance policy, can help you put money away toward future health costs, and keep those expenses down. With a health savings account, you provide pretax earnings to a tax-deferred investment account then make tax-free withdrawals for medical expenses. You'll pay a small annual fee of about $40 for a health savings account from a no-load mutual fund company, like Vanguard or Fidelity. You can contribute up to $3,300 to a health savings account for individual coverage (a maximum of $4,300 if you're fifty-five or older). For families, the limit on contributions is $6,550; $7,550 if you're fifty-five or older. You can find a list of insurers offering these plans at HSA Inside (hsainside.com).

Get up to speed on the Affordable Care Act. The new law will allow you to buy affordable insurance through healthcare exchanges. The federal website Healthcare.gov explains how it works. You can also compare single plans available in your area at the website. Check your state insurance department website too because it might list health insurance choices for residents. Also be sure to ask your doctors which insurance carriers they accept.

If you'll be shopping for an individual health policy, compare premiums, deductibles and out-of-pocket costs at such websites as eHealth (ehealthinsurance.com), GoHealth (gohealthinsurance .com), Insure.com, and NetQuote (netquote.com). Always check to see if your preferred doctors are in-network before you select a plan. Expect your policy to have an annual deductible of $1,000 up to $5,000 to keep monthly premium costs down.

You also can get a local health insurance agent to shop around on your behalf. Look for one at the National Association of Health Underwriters website (nahu.org).

8. Tap tax incentives and low-cost loans for education and training. If possible, keep your current job while you take the courses you need for your new pursuit. Many employers offer tax-free tuition assistance programs. Seek federal financial aid. There's no age limit for a subsidized loan. Research scholarships and grants at finaid.org. Take advantage of IRS education tax breaks.

9. Set up a self-employed retirement fund. If you're starting a business, moving to a nonprofit, or joining a small firm without an employee retirement plan, open one. Your three main options are SEP-IRA, solo 401(k), and a Simple IRA.

10. Squeeze the most from tax breaks. It's best to seek advice from a good CPA or tax professional when looking to write off job-hunting costs such as résumé preparation, travel for interviews, out-placement fees, moving expenses, and professional association dues. Self-employed shifters may be eligible to take job-related federal tax deductions on Schedule C.

Part II: Getting Physically Fit

You don't have to run a speedy mile or bench-press your weight, but you do need to be in shape when embarking on a new venture. This delivers the strength and mental sharpness you'll need to deal with stress, especially when changing jobs, switching careers, or in fact making any big decisions in your life.

It sounds superficial, but an in-shape and energetic appearance is a bonus in the work world. You have a glow of vibrancy and positivity about you that employers and potential clients will pick up on. No kidding.

When you're fit, it impacts your entire psyche and it shows. Get yourself into a routine to work out on a regular basis. Enroll in a yoga class or try it at home. There are a wide variety of yoga formats to choose from these days. Join a gym if that gives you the structure to get going. Or get into the habit of walking at least a half hour at a time, say three or four times a week.

Swimming is a low-impact workout that's great for your cardio-vascular health, too. Seek out a pool at the Y in your town, at a nearby hotel, or at a local high school that's open for workouts from the public. (For example, the Olympic-size pool at the Woodrow Wilson Aquatic Center, located in the public high school near where I live in Washington, DC, is open and free to the public every day, year round.) To use the Y facilities, or one at a hotel, you will probably need to join and pay a membership fee.

I know that part of getting financially fit is paring unnecessary costs, but when it comes to your health, it's worth it. Do shop to get the best deals though.

One easy way to get in a routine is to buy a comfortable pair of walking shoes. It eliminates one excuse right off the bat. I love my sneakers. And I set them to the right of the front door, so they're there when I'm ready to hit the road. Even looking at the shoes as I come and go reminds me, not so subliminally, that I need to keep at it.

I like to walk my Labrador retriever, Zena, briskly for at least four miles a few times a week and shorter distances the other days. She requires walks twice a day. The old adage, a tired dog is a good dog, is a truism in my house, so she keeps me moving.

But you might prefer finding a personal trainer to keep you accountable and working it. Zena has happily accepted this role as overseer and greets me daily with a firm steady gaze and leash in her mouth.

And don't forget to pay attention to a healthy diet. Not to get preachy, but you are what you eat. Smart nutritious eating will boost your energy level and give your skin and hair a healthy glow. For example, I keep a bag of tiny, sweet clementines handy to grab in lieu of M&M's, a childhood habit I have had trouble breaking.

Also be sure to drink lots of water—eight glasses a day is the recommended amount, and more if you're active. I always reach for a glass of water when I'm at the office or home, and request it at restaurants instead of soda.

You know all of this, but it bears repeating. Good nutrition and eating vitamin-dense food boosts immunity and fights illness-causing toxins. It can lower your risk of heart disease, high blood pressure, type 2 diabetes, and more. Plus a proper diet can help keep your weight in shape, too.

Moreover, key nutrients will help keep your mental prowess charged. I recommend that you consume a variety of fruits, leafy green vegetables like spinach and kale, and fish and nuts packed with omega-3 fatty acids. You will have more energy and look better to boot. Talk about a confidence builder.

As with getting financially fit, to get physically fit you should set goals for how much you want to exercise or the amount of weight you'd like to lose to feel good about yourself. Be sure to establish a regular sleeping and eating pattern. I am an early bird, so my day runs from 5:30 to 6 a.m. to 10 to 11 p.m. and no eating after 8 p.m. most days. This schedule takes discipline, but my body gets the rest it needs.

Maintaining a healthy lifestyle should be nonnegotiable and will give you the tools to move through your career transition and bounce back from the inevitable challenges ahead.

Also, I always take the time for an annual checkup with my family doctor and I recommend you do, too. It's a great way to track your cholesterol, blood sugar, and vitamin and mineral levels and discuss any issues you might have on your mind from weight to intermittent pings and pangs. I figure, my car gets regular oil changes and under the hood checks, I should, too.

Part III: Getting Spiritually Fit

I'm not getting all woo woo on you here. And to be clear, I'm not talking about finding religion per se. Although there is certainly nothing wrong with that, if it works for you.

What I suggest to people going through a transition is to find a space where they can get away from the stress and fears that go hand in hand with making changes in their lives. Anxiety and stress are part of the package, but you can seek out ways to cope with it in a positive fashion.

There's a trove of research that shows how meditation and mindfulness can improve the brain's focus and concentration and your overall state of health. For instance, you might want to check out books and more from Deepak Chopra, the founder of the Chopra Foundation (choprafoundation.org).

Chopra writes and lectures about the benefits of meditation and how it can slow your heart rate and normalize blood pressure. Advocates say it can boost your immune system and help you produce fewer stress hormones like adrenaline and cortisol. Moreover, like exercise, it often sparks the brain to release neurotransmitters such as dopamine, serotonin, and endorphins that boost feelings of well-being.

Simply put, mind/body balance helps you calmly roll with the punches, and teaches you to listen quietly to the inner voice that can guide your decisions. Joining a meditation group might be the ticket for you.

Chopra's mantra is that meditation improves health and vitality and enhances the power of the brain. And I agree.

Some other popular ways to slow down and get out of your own head are tai chi and yoga. But there are a host of creative outlets out there, say, listening to music or painting, or gardening. For me, it's horseback riding. When I am cantering down to a jump or loping through a field aboard my wonderful mare, nothing matters but what lies ahead and the pure joy of what I am doing—flying.

We all need a place to go that allows us to lose ourselves, where all the day-to-day work stresses and personal challenges disappear. It is in those times that we are "of the moment" right where we are.

The pure simplicity of it is remarkably freeing. These escape hatches allow our stress to dissipate and our energy to return. Those time-outs can be ephemeral, so snatch, savor, and repeat. Even long walks with your dog can do the trick—walking my dog gives me balance.

Finally, taking time to volunteer and give back to someone or a cause can help you place your own challenges into a realistic perspective and take you outside of your everyday stresses. I have found that this especially provides the karma you need to push on toward your new goals with a sense of calm and purpose.

AFTERWORD

Changing your work life can be risky, but as you've seen from the people you met in these pages, it can be a successful risk—and even more so, a truly satisfying one.

If you've lost your job and are dealing with a second act as a necessity, it's crucial that you don't act out of rashness and fear but rather from knowledge of how you can use this life-changing event to your advantage. True, you may not have the luxury of savings socked away to tide you over while you gain traction in your new work. And you may not have a limitless time horizon before you need to start earning enough to support you and your family.

But, in reality, this may very well be the perfect time to move into a job that means something to you. With the cushion provided by a severance or early-retirement package, grab hold of your chance to try something you have always dreamed of doing, even if it isn't on your time table, but your ex-employer's whim.

We all wrestle with just what it is we're looking for in our job and life. How many times have you been told life is short and not to waste it? To make a complete turn, though, usually takes spirit, strength, and a thirst to find meaning in this life. Not everyone is hardwired for that kind of transformation.

If you've finished this book with a gnawing sense of excitement in your belly for the possibilities out there, you most certainly are one of the lucky ones.

No two paths are the same. Each person I interviewed was faced with a different set of challenges. But their success stories reveal common threads.

Many of these men and women were spurred to discover what really matters to them and transform their work (and, in turn, personal) lives by a crisis or loss that starkly revealed the fleeting nature of a life. No one acted impulsively. They paused. They planned. They bypassed helter-skelter approaches, and pursued prudent, well-researched moves.

Each person set flexible time horizons for his or her venture to make it. If necessary, they added the essential skills and degrees before they made the leap. They often apprenticed or volunteered beforehand. They reached out to their networks of social and professional contacts to ask for help and guidance.

They downsized and planned their financial lives in order to be able to afford a cut in pay or the cost of a startup. Several were fortunate to have had the cushion of a spouse's steady income or had some outside investments, retirement savings, and pensions in place to ease the transition to their new line of work.

But what really sticks with me is that they all share a clear confidence in the direction they have taken, never second-guessing their choice. They collectively work longer hours, but it doesn't matter. They only wish they had done it sooner.

And that says it all.

Good luck!

Ideas for Further Reading

There are scores of great books aimed at changing careers midlife. Here are a few I recommend, but this is by no means the ultimate list. There are always new books coming along. But the ones I list will certainly get you started on your research and provide you with innovative ideas, inspiration, and guidance for finding your next great job.

BOOKS

Alboher, Marci. *The Encore Career Handbook: How to Make a Living and a Difference in the Second Half of Life.* Workman, 2012.

Alboher, Marci. *One Person/Multiple Careers: The Original Guide to the Slash Career.* HeyMarci, 2012.

Astor, Bart. *AARP Roadmap for the Rest of Your Life: Smart Choices about Money, Health, Work, Lifestyle... and Pursuing Your Dreams.* Wiley, 2013.

Bateson, Mary Catherine. *Composing a Further Life.* Knopf, 2010.

Bolles, Richard Nelson. *What Color Is Your Parachute? 2014: A Practical Manual for Job-Hunters and Career-Changers.* Ten Speed Press, 2013.

Bornstein, David. *How to Change the World: Social Entrepreneurs and the Power of New Ideas.* Oxford University Press, 2007.

Carstensen, Laura. *A Long Bright Future: An Action Plan for a Lifetime of Happiness, Health, and Financial Security.* Broadway, 2009.

Collamer, Nancy. *Second-Act Careers: 50+ Ways to Profit from Your Passions During Semi-Retirement.* Ten Speed Press, 2013.

Cullinane, Jan. *The Single Woman's Guide to Retirement.* Wiley, 2012.

Dearie, John and Courtney Geduldig. *Where the Jobs Are: Entrepreneurship and the Soul of the American Economy.* Wiley, 2013.

DiVecchio, Patricia. *Evolutionary Work: Unleashing Your Potential in Extraordinary Times.* Pearhouse Press, 2010.

Frankel, Bruce. *What Should I Do with the Rest of My Life? True Stories of Finding Success, Passion, and New Meaning in the Second Half of Life.* Avery, 2010.

Freedman, Marc. *The Big Shift: Navigating the New Stage Beyond Midlife.* Public Affairs, 2011.

Freedman, Marc. *Encore: Finding Work That Matters in the Second Half of Life.* Public Affairs, 2008.

Hannon, Kerry. *Great Jobs for Everyone 50+: Finding Work That Keeps You Happy and Healthy . . . and Pays the Bills.* Wiley, 2012.

Heath, Chip and Dan Heath. *Switch: How to Change Things When Change Is Hard.* Broadway, 2010.

Hewlett, Sylvia Ann. *Forget a Mentor, Find a Sponsor: The New Way to Fast-Track Your Career.* Harvard Business Review Press, 2013.

Johnson, Tory. *Spark & Hustle: Launch and Grow Your Small Business Now.* Berkeley, 2012.

Kunen, James S. *Diary of a Company Man: Losing a Job, Finding a Life.* Lyons Press, 2012.

Lawrence-Lightfoot, Sara. *The Third Chapter: Passion, Risk, and Adventure in the 25 Years After 50.* Farrar, Straus, & Giroux, 2009.

Leider, Richard J. and Alan M. Webber. *Life Reimagined: Discovering Your New Life Possibilities.* Berrett-Koehler, 2013.

Life Planning Network. *Live Smart After 50!* Life Planning Network, 2013.

Lore, Nicholas. *The Pathfinder: How to Choose or Change Your Career for a Lifetime of Satisfaction and Success.* Fireside, 2012.

Miller, Mark. *The Hard Times Guide to Retirement Security: Practical Strategies for Money, Work, and Living.* Bloomberg Press/Wiley, 2010.

Newman, Rick. *Rebounders: How Winners Pivot from Setback to Success.* Ballantine, 2012.

Palmer, Kimberly. *The Economy of You: Discover Your Inner Entrepreneur and Recession-Proof Your Life.* AMACOM, 2014.

Pauley, Jane. *Your Life Calling: Reimagining the Rest of Your Life.* Simon & Schuster, 2014.

Pink, Daniel. *Drive: The Surprising Truth about What Motivates Us.* Riverhead, 2009.

Salpeter, Miriam and Hannah Morgan. *Social Networking for Business Success: Turn Your Ideas into Income.* LearningExpress, 2013.

Salpeter, Miriam. *Social Networking for Career Success: Using Online Tools to Create a Personal Brand.* LearningExpress, 2011.

Schawbel, Dan. *Promote Yourself: The New Rules for Career Success.* St. Martin's Press, 2013.

Sedlar, Jeri and Rick Miners. *Don't Retire, Rewire: 5 Steps to Fulfilling Work That Fuels Your Passion, Suits Your Personality, and Fills Your Pocket.* 2nd ed. Alpha, 2007.

Taylor, Roberta K. and Dorian Mintzer. *The Couple's Retirement Puzzle: 10 Must-Have Conversations for Transitioning to the Second Half of Life.* Lincoln Street Press, 2011.

Tieger, Paul D. and Barbara Barron-Tieger. *Do What You Are: Discover the Perfect Career for You Through the Secrets of Personality Type.* Little, Brown, 2007.

Transition Network and Gail Rentsch. *Smart Women Don't Retire—They Break Free.* Springboard Press, 2008.

Walton, Mark S. *Boundless Potential: Transform Your Brain, Unleash Your Talents, Reinvent Your Work in Midlife and Beyond.* McGraw-Hill, 2012.

WEBSITES

Nonprofits

Bridgespan.org: includes the Nonprofit Jobs Center, which lists positions, including paid part-time and full-time jobs.

Cgcareers.org: recruits for nonprofit careers at management level.

Change.org: how to build a grassroots campaign and fundraise for a nonprofit and more.

Councilofnonprofits.org: network of state and regional nonprofit associations serving more than twenty thousand organizations.

Encore.org: go-to site for anyone interested in a career with social meaning and purpose; includes a listing of nonprofit job opportunities.

GuideStar.org: leading source on nonprofit organizations.

Idealist.org: provides leads to more than ten thousand job opportunities nationwide in the nonprofit sector.

Independentsector.org: has research and resources of over six hundred charities, foundations, corporations, and individuals.

Philanthropy.com/jobs: job listings, primarily in foundations.

For Job Seekers

AARPworksearch.org: AARP Foundation's WorkSearch Information Network, which covers each phase of the job search, from beginning to accepting a job.

AARP.org/work: offers news, resources, and how-to help, plus the biennial list of Best Employers for Workers Over 50.

Careerbuilder.com: extensive overall career site.

Careeronestop.org: offers career resources to job seekers.

Coolworks.com: database of seasonal jobs, amusement park jobs, and more.

Enrge.us: helps retired federal, state, and local government employees find new employment.

Erieri.com: provides free salary information for both for-profit and nonprofit organizations by industry and geographic location as well as cost-of-living data.

Experiencecorps.org: geared to Americans over fifty-five who want to tutor and mentor in underserved schools.

Execsearches.com: job board focused on government, nonprofit, education, and health openings.

Execunet.com: network of senior-level retired executives.

Flexjobs.com: subscription-based job board for listing prescreened openings for freelancers, telecommuters, and more.

Glassdoor.com: jobs and career community that offers an inside look at jobs and companies, salary information, and so on.

Govloop.com: connects more than fifty thousand federal, state, and local government workers with job posts.

Greenbiz.com: comprehensive green business news and information site with a section dedicated to environmentally friendly jobs.

Indeed.com: online jobs listing and search engine that aggregates thousands of jobs listings from multiple sites.

Job-hunt.org: comprehensive list of job search resources and links to employer recruiting pages.

Jobmonkey.com: features seasonal and summer gigs.

Jobs4point0.com: focuses on job seekers ages forty and over.

Monster.com: large general jobs website with a special section for older workers.

Nextavenue.org: great source of information and advice for finding a job, switching fields, and starting a business after fifty.

Ourpublicservice.org: nonprofit that works with federal agencies for place workers.

Payscale.com: offers salary data for a broad sweep of jobs.

Peacecorps.gov: offers some paid volunteering overseas in areas such as education, health, business, and information and communication technology.

Philanthropy.com/jobs: provides a listing of jobs, primarily in foundations.

Primecb.com: Careerbuilder.com's section for experienced workers.

Ratracerebellion.com: geared for work-at-home opportunities.

Reserveinc.org: an innovative resource that matches older professionals with nonprofits in several cities, including Baltimore, Miami, and New York.

Retiredbrains.com: online job board that connects to thousands of jobs for those over fifty; a resource center on other retirement-related issues, from continuing education to healthcare to dealing with grief.

Retireeworkforce.com: provides job postings and résumé services, plus a database with flexible, seasonal, and full-time positions specifically for more experienced candidates.

Retirementjobs.com: geared toward fifty-plus job seekers.

Salary.com: free source for salary comparisons by city and job.

Seniorentrepreneurshipworks.org: nonprofit organization designed to engage, empower, and connect would-be entrepreneurs over fifty-five.

Seniorjobbank.org: a career site for boomers and seniors with an active jobs board.

Seniors4hire.org: job seekers can submit a résumé, post a description of their model job, or apply for posted jobs.

Seniorserviceamerica.org: federally funded programs that provide temporary or full-time jobs with local, state, and federal government agencies.

Simplyhired.com: large jobs database.

Thenonprofittimes.com/jobs: fast-growing jobs board for job seekers; reports on charitable organizations' salaries and benefits.

Usajobs.gov: official website for federal jobs.

Vault.com: job-hunting site with a range of postings and help.

Vcn.org/healthcare: U.S. Department of Labor–sponsored site that provides help finding healthcare jobs and training programs.

Workforce50.com: offers employment and career change resources.

Yourencore.com: connects retired scientists, engineers, and product developers with consulting and short-term assignments.

Continuing Education

Encore.org/colleges: listing of over-fifty programs at community colleges around the country.

Fastweb.com: search engine for research scholarships and grants for older students offered by associations, colleges, religious groups, and foundations.

Finaid.org: free resource for objective and unbiased information, advice, and tools about financial aid.

Irs.gov: information about educational tax breaks in Publication 970.

Nasfaa.org: site of the National Association of Student Financial Aid Administrators.

Osher.net: home of Osher Lifelong Learning Institute.

Plus50.aacc.nche.edu: site of the Plus 50 Program from the American Association of Community Colleges.

Studentaid.ed.gov: federal financial aid to offset education costs; no age limit to apply; available to part-time students.

Small Businesses

SBA.gov: complete small-business resources from loans to franchising to tips on starting a small company, from the U.S. Small Business Administration.

Score.org: nonprofit association dedicated to educating entrepreneurs and the formation, growth, and success of small businesses nationwide.

Startupnation.com: site dedicated to small-business groups.

Crowd Funding

Angel.co: can link you up with angel investors.

Indiegogo.com: can link you up with angel investors.

Kickstarter.com: a site that allows individuals and organizations to raise funds for a project through an online platform.

Rockthepost.com: free network that helps entrepreneurs meet professionals and investors who can help via funds, time, or materials.

Social Networking

Facebook.com: free online social network service that lets you connect with friends and businesses.

Googleplus.com: free social network that allows you to share articles and YouTube links with friends, hold online chats via hangouts, and more.

Linkedin.com: online professional network with more than 225 million members. You can create a professional profile or online résumé, look for jobs, join work-related groups, network, post articles, and more.

Twitter.com: free online social network that lets you share and read messages limited to 140 characters.

Volunteering

Handsonnetwork.org: skills-based volunteer activation arm of Points of Light with 250 community-action centers.

Lawyerswithoutborders.org: directs legal pro bono services around the world.

1-800-volunteer.org: database of more than twenty-six thousand projects nationwide.

Onlinevolunteering.org: database of volunteer opportunities with organizations that serve communities in developing countries; sponsored by the United Nations.

Operationhope.org: for volunteers with a background in the financial industry to work with victims of hurricanes and other disasters, offering online financial and budget counseling.

Taprootfoundation.org: organizes teams of professionals for pro bono consulting with nonprofits in seven cities; fields include finance, marketing, and information technology.

Volunteer.gov: one-stop shop for public service volunteer projects sponsored by the federal government.

Volunteermatch.org: more than fifty-four thousand listings nationwide; extensive searchable database of projects.

Fundraising

AFPnet.org: site of the Association of Fundraising Professionals.

Foundationcenter.org: site of the Foundation Center.

Career Coaches

ACPinternational.org: site of the Association of Career Professionals.

Coachu.com: site of a provider of coach training courses.

Coachfederation.org: a nonprofit organization that provides a network for coaches. It also offers individual credentialing courses.

NCDA.org: site of the National Career Development Association.

PARW.com: site of the Professional Association of Résumé Writers and Career Coaches.

WABCcoaches.com: site of the Worldwide Association of Business Coaches.

Franchising

Franchise.org: organization of franchisers, franchisees, and suppliers.

Franchisee.org: national trade association of franchisees and dealers with over seven thousand members.

Franchiseregistry.com: searchable data by franchise or by industry.

SBA.gov: site of the U.S. Small Business Administration; features a small-business planner section.

Social Entrepreneurs

Ashoka.org: Ashoka Fellows are provided with living stipends, professional support, and access to a global network of peers in more than sixty countries.

Echoinggreen.org: two-year fellowship program to help entrepreneurs develop new solutions to society's most difficult problems.

Globalgiving.com: enables individuals and companies to find and support social and economic development projects around the world.

Investorscircle.net: lists angel investors, professional venture capitalists, foundations, and others who invest in projects addressing social and environmental issues.

Schwabfound.org: provides scholarship opportunities to the best executive education to selected social entrepreneurs.

Skollfoundation.org: helps social entrepreneurs better communities around the world.

ACKNOWLEDGMENTS

I am indebted to so many people for their contributions, support, and wisdom:

I am most grateful to my "second acters," who shared their stories, inspiration, and precious time with me. You're making a difference not only in your own lives but in others' journeys as well. I am in awe.

Many career experts lent me their time and deep knowledge as I explored in-depth the world of career transition. But there were three pros who were always there to take a phone call, respond to an email, or point me in the right direction.

Marc Freedman, the founder and CEO of Encore.org, never fails to inspire me with his clear vision of the future, as well as his love for Americana roots music.

Betsy Werley is a woman I connected with the moment I met her. She boldly set the Transition Network firmly on an ever-expanding path to engage and connect women over fifty, who are navigating change. At the time this book was going to press, Betsy was moving on to a new stage in her working life, as an Encore Innovation Fellow at Encore.org.

And a final tip of the hat to my favorite career coach Beverly Jones—I am beholden.

The "Second Acts" column I created and developed for *U.S. News & World Report* was sparked by the vision and skilled editorial touch of *U.S. News & World Report* executive editor Tim Smart. Thanks, Tim, for giving me the opportunity to run with this concept and meet these remarkable individuals.

If not for my brother, Michael Hannon—who recruited from his deep network of friends and colleagues in my hometown of Pittsburgh, Pennsylvania, the first two career changers who recounted their successful transitions for my column—this path into second careers might never have taken flight. Mike, thanks for all your support and big-brother advice along the way.

My deep appreciation to my literary agent, Linda Konner, whose enthusiasm and insight made it possible for this book to be published initially in hardback by Chronicle Books and now in the revised and updated paperback by Berkley Books, a division of Penguin Random House. Thanks for believing in me.

My gratitude to the energetic and visionary Adrienne Avila, my editor at Berkley Books, who keenly recognized the significance of motivating and helping midcareer workers discover ways to take a chance, follow dreams, and forge rewarding new career paths.

I would also like to send a special thanks to Candace B. Levy, who executed a smooth and sharp-eyed copyedit of my manuscript for Berkley Books.

And an appreciation, of course, to Ursula Cary, my editor at Chronicle Books, who knew immediately the magic of helping people follow their dreams.

As always, I prevailed on my husband, Cliff, to critique my

drafts, and he cheerfully and thoughtfully never hesitated to do so. Thank you.

To the entire Bonney family—Paul, Pat, Christine, Mike, Caitlin, and Shannon—for always carrying me under your wing and allowing me to share in those blissful days at your villa in St. John, where I started writing this book.

To Jane Kelso, who opened the doors to the joys of Rappahannock County and the creative forces that propelled my days of writing there amid the quiet and mountain vistas.

To my trainer, Jonelle Mullen Stern, and the crew at TuDane Farm, who offered me respite from deadlines atop a horse cantering down to jumps or roaming along pine-needle trails.

To my brother, Jack, who is always there when I need him.

Special shouts to those essential "have-my-backers" in the Hannon family—Judy, Brendan, Sean, Conor, Brian, and Charmaine.

Last, to my mother, Marguerite, who never fails to encourage me and to listen, and to my late father, John W. Hannon, who always nourished my dreams: You were right . . . you do have to dream to get there.

And, of course, Zena, what would I do without my four-legged road manager?

INDEX

ABOUT THE AUTHOR

Kerry Hannon is a bestselling author and Washington, DC–based career, retirement, and personal finance expert.

Kerry is the author of the national bestseller *Great Jobs for Everyone 50+: Finding Work That Keeps You Happy and Healthy . . . and Pays the Bills* (Wiley, 2012).

Kerry has spent more than twenty-five years covering all aspects of personal finance for the nation's leading media companies, including the *New York Times, Forbes, Money, U.S. News & World Report*, and *USA Today*. She is a nationally recognized authority on boomer career transitions and retirement.

She is AARP's Jobs Expert and is the "Great Jobs" columnist for AARP.org.

Kerry is a contributing editor at *Forbes* magazine, is the "Second Verse" columnist for Forbes.com, and is recognized as the Forbes's bard of career transitions and working retirement issues.

She is the PBS website NextAvenue.org expert on career and personal finance for boomer women and writes a weekly column.

She is a Metlife Foundation and New America Media Fellow on Aging.

She is the award-winning author of *What's Next? Follow Your Passion and Find Your Dream Job* (Chronicle Books, 2010).

Kerry is also the author *of Getting Started in Estate Planning* (Wiley), *Suddenly Single: Money Skills for Divorcees and Widows* (Wiley), *Ten Minute Guide to Retirement for Women* (Macmillan), *You and Your Money: A Passage from Debt to Prosperity* (Credit Education Group), and *Trees in a Circle: The Teec Nos Pos Story*.

She has previously served as a staff reporter and personal finance columnist for *USA Today* and as a staff writer and editor for *U.S. News & World Report*, *Money*, *Kiplinger's Personal Finance*, and *Forbes*.

She has appeared as a financial expert on *NBC Nightly News* with Brian Williams as well as on ABC, CBS, Fox, CNBC, CNN, and PBS and has been a guest on numerous radio programs, including National Public Radio.

Kerry received a bachelor of arts degree from Duke University and is currently a member of an editorial board at Duke. She grew up in Pittsburgh, Pennsylvania, and is on a board at her alma mater, Shady Side Academy.

For more, go to kerryhannon.com.